The Lotus &
Caterham Sevens

A collector's guide
by Jeremy Coulter

MOTOR RACING PUBLICATIONS LTD
Unit 6, The Pilton Estate, 46 Pitlake, Croydon CRO 3RY, England

ISBN 0 947981 06 3
First published 1986

Photoset and printed in Great Britain by
Netherwood, Dalton & Company Ltd
Bradley Mills, Huddersfield, West Yorkshire.

The Lotus & Caterham Sevens

Contents

Introduction

The Seven is a remarkable car. Its design is beautifully simple and its makeup draws heavily from the proprietary parts bin. Yet few other cars have come close to it in terms of driver appeal and sheer excitement behind the wheel. It has remained in virtually continuous production since 1957 which represents a truly extraordinary life span, far in excess of that of most other cars and testimony to the Seven's special qualities.

The Seven's survival has been against all odds. Graham Nearn of Caterham Cars calls the Seven a maverick (dictionary definition: one who does not conform) and he's exactly right. It was vintage in appearance back in 1957 with its rudimentary body, cycle wings and minimal equipment. Changing public taste should have killed it off, but didn't. So should changes in taxation or legislation, but neither of these could make the Seven lie down despite successive attempts.

That is not to say that it has been produced with much conviction – until recently. Colin Chapman might happily have let it drop with only 200 or so units built soon after Lotus moved to Cheshunt. For him the Seven was an expedient model that brought in money when it was needed. He was always anxious to move on to the next project; never one to dwell on the past. But within Lotus, the Seven found its niche and simply kept going. It seemed that the end was nigh when production stopped after the factory move to Norfolk, but the temptation of ready cash set production rolling again. Then came the over-selling of the Series 4 Seven, the advent of Value Added Tax, the first fuel crisis and the associated depression which combined ultimately to lead Lotus to axe the car altogether. But still it wouldn't die. Through dogged persistence, Caterham Cars took over manufacture of the Seven, found their feet and made headway through production difficulties and ever tighter legislative restrictions.

There are Sevens for everybody. Aluminium-winged historic racers; screaming Cosworth-powered cars to show off at Classic car events; simple and reliable, yet still exhilaratingly fast basic Ford-engined Sevens for enjoying twisting country lanes in the summer; tuned Twin Cam versions that double as road cars and frighteningly fast racing machines; and then there are brand new Sevens with a choice of engines and the very latest equipment, right up to the 16-valve Cosworth-engined Seven HPC that you can't buy unless you take a high-performance driving course.

In this book I have tried to trace the history of the Seven in as much depth as space permits. Sorting out some of the details has been impossible, simply because production numbers have been so low and there have been so many specification changes. There have also been numerous oddball Sevens, several originating with the factory and others as creations of private owners; some have escaped the net. As a Seven enthusiast and owner myself, I hope that I have managed to convey at least a flavour of the enthusiasm, excitement and humour associated with this 'Legend in its own Lifetime'.

September 1986   JEREMY COULTER

Acknowledgements

I found researching the history of the Seven a tremendously enjoyable task. Almost everyone associated with the car found time to sit and talk about their memories or recount a particularly funny incident involving the car. In fact, humour pervades the Seven story; there was the Lotus Sales Manager who left the road during a demonstration run in a Seven and had to ask the quaking customer to help him lift the car from an earth bank; the classical musician who built a Seven in his loft and then had to take it to bits again to get it down! Then there was the Seven racer who limped his car back from Ireland to Camberley with only top gear and during the course of the journey had a runaway bull leap clean over the car. Or there was the Seven owner who wrote to Lotus asking for a cure for low oil pressure and was advised to cover up the pressure gauge with sticky tape!

For finding the time to 'talk Sevens' let me thank the following in particular. Graham Nearn and David Wakefield of Caterham Cars; Jez Coates, Peter Cooper and Simon Wheeler also of Caterham; Clive Roberts, formerly of Caterham and now working at Lotus; Reg Price of Astap Engineering; Warren King, Financial controller of Lotus Engineering who missed a Board meeting so he could sit and talk about his first Seven; Mike Warner, former head of Lotus Components; Graham Arnold, former Lotus Sales Director and now leading light of Club Lotus; Peter Brand, one-time Lotus Seven fitter and now the longest-serving employee at Lotus; Roy Badcock, one-time foreman of Lotus Components; Brian Luff, buyer of the first customer Seven; Ian Jones, the man who drew the plans for the Seven; Don Gadd and Bob Robinson of Arch Motors; John Derisley, one-time Seven racer; Peter Warr, former Seven owner and now Director of Team Lotus; Fred Bushell, once MD of Lotus; Edward Lewis, recipient of the first ever Seven; David Lazenby, former head of Lotus Components and now of Pace Products; Mike Brotherwood, owner and restorer of Sevens; Frank Coltman, formerly of Progress Chassis and now a restorer of the cars he once built; Hugh Edgley, Lotus enthusiast and owner; and journalist and author Chris Harvey who was a source of endless encouragement during the gestation of this book. Also thanks to the owners who provided the cars shown on the jacket – Mike Brotherwood's restored 1959 S1 Super Seven, Gary Robinson's 1969 1,600cc S4, Graham Nearn's 1968 Twin Cam SS and one of Caterham's demonstrators, a new 1,700cc Supersprint. Thanks too to *Classic Cars* photographer Mike Valente for taking the photograph.

And finally, thanks to the late Colin Chapman himself, who, unbeknown to him, contributed to this book through a taped interview about the Seven organized by Graham Nearn back in 1978.

JEREMY COULTER

CHAPTER 1

Ancestors and parentage

Early days at Lotus

Colin Chapman died on December 16, 1982 aged just 54. At his wake some days later, former Lotus Director, Mike Warner, stood talking with Keith Duckworth, head of Cosworth Engineering. Both men had known Chapman for years. Renowned as a man of few words and one who does not lavish praise unduly, Duckworth looked down into his glass and said 'You know Mike, I think Colin Chapman was the cleverest man I ever knew.' That was praise indeed from a person of Duckworth's achievement. In saying it he was putting into words the thoughts of most of Chapman's contemporaries as well as those who had owned, driven or admired the cars that Lotus built.

Chapman was indisputably a supremely gifted engineer; if part of his talent was sometimes to make reality of the ideas of others, that is not to belittle his achievements. The idea of a car like the Lotus Seven, created from simple components and with the simplest of bodies, was not startlingly original. But what was unique was the way the design worked so well and has lasted, setting it head and shoulders above others as the archetypal small, high-performance sports car.

Interviewed in 1978, Colin Chapman recalled startlingly little about the Seven, but maybe that was hardly surprising when one considers the number of projects he was involved with in the intervening quarter century. He was never one to reflect on the past. 'When you concern yourself with the past, you stop seeing the future clearly,' he once said. 'I did have a real affection for the Seven, but remember that in all those years we built it, it was really just a bread-and-butter line.'

Bread-and-butter the Seven may have been back in the late 1950s, but it was a crucial factor in the long march of Lotus from Austin Seven Special builder to one of today's most progressive and innovative manufacturers on a world scale.

Without the Seven to fill in the lulls in production of more specialized Lotus models, the young Lotus Engineering company would probably have folded at the first seasonal slump in orders for racing cars. As Lotus grew, moving to successively larger premises, so the Seven started to be produced on a more regular, better organized basis, remaining a small but significant facet in the Lotus model range.

In the wave of post-war enthusiasm for motoring and motor sport Colin Chapman had built the very first Lotus, retrospectively christened the Mark 1, while still at London University during 1948. He cleverly modified a 1930 Austin Seven, working in a garage behind his girlfriend's house in north London. The basic Lotus tenets of lightness and ingenious chassis design were applied as far as possible on this simple car which Chapman used in the only form of motorsport available to him at the time, on muddy and wet trials hills.

The following year, with University over and national service notwithstanding, Chapman turned his mind to the Mark 2 Lotus, which had an Austin Seven chassis the same as his first car, but was rather more specialized and had a body that looked altogether sportier, albeit slightly odd in appearance. The Mark 2 enjoyed a full and quite successful trials season and it proved itself to be no slouch on the race track either.

It was the Mark 3 of 1951 that saw a definite move away from trials. With the wider availability of real circuit racing, the third Lotus was designed primarily with this activity in mind. Running in the competitive 750 formula, this little car began making a

Colin Chapman's talents were not confined to the drawing board, he was a gifted driver too. Here he is in June 1953 driving Adam Currie's Lotus Mark 3B at Silverstone.

name for itself and its driver. Quite often this was Chapman himself demonstrating that he was almost as talented behind the wheel as he was behind the drawing board.

By this time, sufficient people were expressing interest in this new brand of sports car for Chapman to place his vehicle building activities on a slightly more businesslike footing. Thus the Lotus Engineering Co came into being on January 1, 1952 in tiny premises behind the Railway Hotel owned by Chapman's father at 7 Tottenham Lane, Hornsey, London N8, telephone number FITzroy 1777.

Not that this businesslike footing ran to the extent of Colin Chapman's giving up his full-time job with British Aluminium. His ambition was matched by his energy and, after spending the day working in London, he would return to Hornsey to work alongside his then partner Michael Allen and a band of enthusiastic unpaid friends and helpers who willingly gave of their time and skills just to get close to racing cars.

The Mark 4 of 1954 was a successful trials car that further promoted the name of Lotus. Its intended successor was the Mark 5, a 750 formula racer, but it never saw the light of day. Instead, all efforts were diverted into the Mark 6, the first Lotus conceived with series production in mind.

For the first time Colin Chapman sketched out an entirely new chassis rather than one based on the Austin Seven's. The scheme was for a simple yet stiff and light spaceframe with two larger bottom rails. Such an advanced stressed design was a new departure for Lotus and a moonlighting pair of design engineers from nearby aircraft builders De Havilland, Peter Ross and Mac Mackintosh, came in when they could to help with the development of the chassis. Mackintosh's contribution to the stress calculations was particularly significant. Another important moonlighting engineer from De Havilland who was introduced to Hornsey at around this time was Mike Costin. He was to become a key figure in the development of the company.

Working conditions for these draughtsmen-engineers were pretty basic and the lack of space for a drawing office at Hornsey

The Lotus Mark 6 was conceived as a production car right from the start and quickly came to dominate the smaller classes in sports-car racing. One of the most successful Mark 6s was the MG-powered car of Peter Gammon which enjoyed a string of wins in 1954. UPE 9 is now owned by Graham Nearn of Caterham Cars and is often displayed in Caterham's showroom.

meant that much of the work was done at Chapman's house in Barnet. When there was no alternative to tackling some drawing work at Hornsey, there was room above the workshops in the spares loft, reached by a precarious vertical ladder. However, it was a risky business leaving drawings up there and once the whole project nearly foundered when mice gnawed their way into the drawing cabinet and ate the contents!

The prototype Mark 6 chassis was built up by the Progress Chassis Co, based in garages a few doors down from the Lotus works and run by Chapman's friend, John Teychenne. The garages used by Teychenne were at the rear of his father's house and completed chassis were quite often stored on the lawn. Panel beaters Williams and Pritchard occupied one of the sheds at 7 Tottenham Lane and it was they who clothed the bare bones of the new chassis in aluminium and beat out simple front cycle wings, nose cone, rear wings, bonnet and tunnel cover.

Cheap and easily available Ford mechanical parts were hung on this chassis: a reliable 1,172cc Ford Prefect engine provided the motive power. The suspension design was similar to the system used on earlier Lotus models with a modified Ford axle at the front, divided to form a simple swing axle, not ideal by any

means, but cheap and effective.

The Ford Prefect may have been a fairly pedestrian vehicle but the combination of lightness and clever chassis design made the Lotus Mark 6 a very lively performer, ideally suited to the race track but just as much at home as everyday transport for the young, or young-at-heart, sporting motorist. Right from its creation in 1953 the Lotus Mark 6 became a familiar sight on Britain's racetracks and it wasn't long before what were initially known as 'Lotus Replicas' were offered for general sale in kit form. A Reading-based company, Buckler, run by Derek Buckler, offered cars in kit form before Lotus, but the kits that Chapman offered were more comprehensive, including most of the special parts needed, and not just the chassis.

It was an established principle that people who wanted a car primarily for sporting purposes could build a 'one-off' for themselves by accumulating the component parts and in doing so they would not attract purchase tax. At 25% of the purchase price this was a very important consideration. Production of the Mark 6 really came on stream in 1954, still in a fairly informal setting. However, enthusiastic Nobby Clarke, initially a 'volunteer', started working full-time to run the production side of the business. Even so, the happy band of unpaid helpers was still very much in evidence in the Hornsey workshops. Never one not to make use of people's enthusiasm, Chapman established the volunteer-based Team Lotus alongside Lotus Engineering, to develop and run the works racing cars.

As a student with digs in Hornsey, John Derisley, later a well-known and successful Lotus racer, was one of the many who spent spare time lending a hand at Hornsey. His enthusiasm for Lotus had been fired when he had seen Colin Chapman in the Mark 2 leading Dudley Gahagan's Bugatti in a widely reported race at the Silverstone Eight Clubs meeting back in 1950. After wandering in to the Hornsey workshops one day, Derisley found himself enlisted as a Team Lotus helper. He recalls an atmosphere of tremendous activity and apparent confusion. Of Chapman himself Derisley saw little at this time. When the 'boss' wasn't attending to his daytime job at British Aluminium, he was often to be found seated at his drawing board at home, having done a few hours in the workshop before going off to work in the morning.

Chapman became something of a legend at British Aluminium, not least by turning up for important meetings looking terribly windswept after rushing there in a Mark 6. On one occasion he arrived soaked to the skin having been caught in a cloudburst. A complete change of clothing had to be found for him before he could join the meeting.

With production of the Mark 6 going full swing, Chapman's thoughts moved towards the model that would bear the designation Mark 8. He had already allocated the 7 slot on his drawing board to a single-seater racer design tackled as a commission for the Clairmonte brothers. Chapman himself recalled the design as being based around an Alta engine, but others recall the Clairmontes' car as having an ERA unit earmarked for it. Anyway, the car was never completed by Lotus and Chapman handed it over to the brothers who finished it themselves and christened it the Clairmonte Special. With the designation '7' semi-used, Chapman opted to jump straight on to Mark 8 for the next Lotus. Besides which, Mark 7 would come in handy for a Mark 6 replacement should one ever be needed.

The Mark 8 of 1954 developed the Mark 6's chassis design further and Mike Costin's brother Frank, yet another De Havilland employee, came up with a wind-cheating full-width body which gave the car easy 100mph-plus capability. For the following season, 1955, the Marks 9 and 10 were introduced, developing the Mark 8 design still further. 1955 was also a significant year as both Colin Chapman and Mike Costin started working for the company full-time. Costin took charge of a newly created Racing Engines division for which a corner of the already overcrowded workshop was found.

By 1955 around 100 examples of the Mark 6 had been built and the model was still dominating its class in racing. Similarly the Marks 8, 9 and 10 were notching up success after success. Never one to rest on his laurels, Chapman started to wind down production of the Mark 6 in late 1955 to concentrate on developing the Eleven ('Mark' was dropped after the 10). A handful of Mark 6s were built after that date to use up spare chassis and customer cars would come back for repair from time to time.

Mac Mackintosh and Colin Chapman had been spending long hours calculating stresses and experimenting with chassis configurations to see what were the smallest and lightest tubes that could be used and still give a stiff chassis. The Eleven of 1956 was the product of these studies and had a light, uniformly triangulated spaceframe in which the main tubes were 1in diameter of 18 or 20 gauge steel, with ¾in secondary tubes. It was an immediate racing success and eager buyers formed an orderly queue at Hornsey. By now production was becoming better organized with the company expanding to fill what little space was available and taking on more full-time staff.

With such wide-ranging success in sports-car racing it was logical that Lotus should move into single seaters. The Formula 2 Twelve, strongly influenced by the Eleven, was a first step in that direction. The influence worked both ways, however, and when an updated Eleven was introduced in 1957, it featured the new wishbone-type independent front suspension that had been developed for the Twelve.

In early 1957 Team Lotus moved into their own workshop at Hornsey and a prefabricated garage put up to house a special engine shop. Lack of planning permission meant that the Team Lotus transporter had to be parked across the yard entrance to keep out prying eyes while the new building was hastily erected. Once in place, chassis and boxes were casually stacked round it and it blended in so well that no-one ever noticed. Later in 1957,

The Seven was the spiritual successor to the Mark 6 but the chassis was more closely related to the Eleven, shown here in two forms. The Climax engine and de Dion rear suspension of the Eleven Le Mans, left, was too expensive for all but a few special Sevens, and the production cars had the live axle of the Eleven Club model, right.

and with rather more heed to planning regulations, a new office block and sales department was built at the front of the yard. However, the facilities at 7 Tottenham Lane still didn't run to toilets and when nature beckoned, staff could be seen making their way across the railway tracks behind the works to pay British Railways a penny for the use of the conveniences on Hornsey station.

Right up to the Series 2 version of the Eleven, Colin Chapman had been drawing heavily upon the services of Mac Mackintosh and Peter Ross, but in January 1957 he employed his first full-time draughtsman, Ian Jones, whom he had met while doing consultancy work on the Vanwall GP car for Vandervell. In the best Lotus tradition, Jones had started by moonlighting for Lotus, working at Chapman's home. But with the offer of £10 per week and a Chapman promise; 'Come and work for me and I'll

make you a star,' Jones needed little urging to join up full time.

Initially Jones was based at Chapman's house in Barnet, but the need to be near the workshop led to his being installed in the loft at Hornsey. As he recalls, 'The fact that I was taken on as a draughtsman meant very little really. I drew, but I also went and fetched sandwiches when we were up all night, cut pieces of chassis tube and made brackets on the bench. If these parts worked on the job, I'd go back upstairs and draw them. It was a fairly practical set-up at that stage. You can forget the idea of clean white shirts and a real drawing office.' For services rendered, both Ross and Mackintosh were sold Series 2 Elevens at a knock-down price and they were well pleased.

With the Eleven selling well and more ambitious racing car projects in the pipeline, Jones was able to get his teeth into a rather more straightforward project that Colin Chapman had up

The Climax-engined Formula 2 Lotus Twelve single seater provided the wishbone front suspension design first for the Series 2 Eleven, replacing the swing-axle layout of all the earlier cars, and then for the Seven. A single transverse link formed the upper wishbone, fore-and-aft location being cleverly provided by the anti-roll bar.

his sleeve, the long-delayed replacement for the Mark 6.

That the market existed for a Mark 6 replacement was highlighted by the fact that the second-hand value of the Mark 6 remained remarkably high two years after the model had been dropped. There was also a high level of customer enquiries about a Mark 6 replacement and Sales Manager Colin Bennett was keen to have a road car to sell. Most customers would undoubtedly have loved an Eleven, but at £1,511 for the cheapest version it was way beyond the means of the average motorist.

At an internal level, the growing staff at Hornsey, and thus the need for a degree of financial stability, increased the appeal of a product that wasn't subject to the same seasonal demand pattern as racing cars. The idea that Chapman formulated was for a car

that could be built by the racing department in the late summer and early winter when no decision had been made as to what racing models would be built for the following season. Around January or February the works would stop building the 'fill-in' and start frantically building racing cars once again, and so on. That was the theory – but somehow it never worked out exactly like that.

Chapman was also looking to the future. He knew that Lotus could never grow really big simply by producing racing cars; becoming a 'real' manufacturer of sporting road cars was his aim and the Seven seemed a good way to start, particularly as the innovative Fourteen, otherwise known as the Elite, was proving much more difficult to develop than had been anticipated.

CHAPTER 2

Four-wheeled motorcycle

Design of the Seven

The Lotus Seven was to be primarily a road-going sports car rather than a racing car. However, the buyer that Colin Chapman had in mind was the person who would drive the car to work in the week and then at weekends, use it in the less serious forms of motor sport – hillclimbs, sprints and club races. But first and foremost it was conceived for the road. Hand in hand with the Elite, it was to be Chapman's first step on the way to becoming a fully-fledged manufacturer.

Colin Chapman had a taker for the first Seven even before it was built. He was Edward Lewis, the energetic proprietor of Westover Shoes, manufacturers of racing footwear, and he was already a well-known Lotus racer. He had started with a Mark 6 in 1953 and progressed to a works-assisted Mark 9 for the 1955 season. Lewis considered buying an Eleven for the 1956 season but felt he might be getting a little old for serious racing and instead set about creating a car to his own specification that he thought would be ideally suited to hillclimbing, which was his particular passion.

The Edward Lewis special was based on a Mark 6 chassis but fitted with Mark 9 running gear: it had a de Dion rear end with inboard drum brakes and was powered by a 1,100cc Climax engine. Williams and Pritchard panelled the body to Lewis's own design but had it back a week later to widen the rear bodywork after Lewis had discovered that the Mark 9's track was wider than the Mark 6 and the de Dion wouldn't fit. Once this and other teething problems had been overcome, the car was road registered FVV 877 and made its competition debut in the West Essex Speed Trials on September 14, 1956.

Colin Chapman had been preoccupied with other things while Lewis was building his special, otherwise he would have told him that a Mark 9 de Dion was wider than a Mark 6 live axle. However, once the car started notching up successes, Chapman started to take note, even though he was not particularly enthusiastic about hillclimbing and sprinting. Still, he appreciated its popularity among the club fraternity, saw a potential market and decided to install Lewis in a 'real' Lotus rather that a Lotus-derived special. The deal he proposed was that as a straight swap for the special, Lewis would be given the prototype Lotus Seven to be built as soon as possible, which he would continue to run in hillclimbs and sprints but under the Team Lotus banner.

Lewis duly handed over the special in early 1957. It languished in a lock-up at Hornsey and was tended to by Graham Hill until it was sold complete to a customer living in Kenya, although the registration documents remained at Hornsey.

Meanwhile Lewis waited for his new car. The incubation period lengthened weekly but Lewis didn't mind one bit because in the meantime Chapman allowed him to borrow the works Elevens for his sport. Lewis: 'I didn't mind at all about the delay because I soon discovered that well-prepared works cars are always quicker than the standard ones available to even keen amateur builders or tuners.' In those works cars, Lewis enjoyed nine first places in sprints and hillclimbs that season.

By the late spring of 1957, Colin Chapman at last found the time to turn his thoughts to the new car, maybe even drawing a little inspiration for it from the special that Lewis had built. Working at his drawing board at his home in Barnet, Chapman quickly put his thoughts down on paper and came up with the

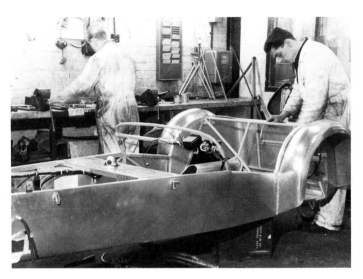

A view of the Edward Lewis special built by Lewis mainly for sprinting and hillclimbing in the 1956/1957 season. The car was built round a Mark 6 chassis with slightly widened rear end to accommodate a Mark 9 de Dion with drum brakes. Power came from a 1,100cc Coventry Climax engine. Lewis's car was beautifully constructed although it should be said that he was not the first person to build a special of this specification. However, this particular one seemed to attract Colin Chapman's eye and led to Lewis being offered the very first Seven, as and when it was built, as a straight swap for the special.

Work on the first Seven was not started until the spring of 1957 and Edward Lewis did not take delivery of his car until September of that year. This photograph taken during 1957 shows a very early Seven chassis being assembled in the Hornsey workshops.

overall plan for the Lotus Seven. He was later to reflect: 'There wasn't much to it really, it was all pretty well-known stuff, the sort of thing you could dash off in a weekend.'

Those plans that he produced in the spring of 1957 were sufficient for Progress Chassis to come up with the frame for the first example of the new car which Williams and Pritchard panelled in aluminium, beating out simple yet attractive wings and clip-over bonnet. Roy Badcock, who was the foreman of Lotus Engineering in 1957 under Manager Nobby Clarke, recalls the pre-production prototype being built in much the same way as a normal racing prototype. Chapman himself recalled, 'Like most projects at that time, you could do the basic calculations, lay out a chassis, lay out the suspension, knock it out sort of thing, and there it was!'

Essentially the chassis of the new car was a cross between a Mark 6 and a Series 2 Eleven. The resemblance to the Eleven chassis was mainly in the method of construction. Lay the two side by side and they look very different, not least in that the

This shot of an almost-completed Seven at Hornsey is quite possibly Edward Lewis's car in its final stages. It is definitely not the Jack Richards car as that did not have a speedometer whereas this one does, mounted on the left of the dash.

Another Hornsey shot taken later in 1957 which shows one of the earliest production chassis fresh from the Progress Chassis Co being wired up and fitted out.

frontwards taper of the Seven's chassis started at the scuttle rather than part way into the engine bay. The arrangement of the tubes at the front and rear also differed as the new car wasn't to have as much bodywork as the Eleven, but in respect of the design of the centre section, tunnel structure, axle mountings and scuttle, the Seven's chassis was similar to that of the Eleven.

The chassis was panelled in an open-wheel style reminiscent of the Mark 6. However, it had an altogether sleeker appearance. Mindful of the publicity job that Lewis would be performing, Chapman equipped the prototype Seven with the rear suspension of the 'Le Mans' specification S2 Eleven, with a de Dion axle and inboard disc brakes. There were disc brakes at the front too. The front suspension, also as per the S2 Eleven, came from the single-seater Twelve. The engine chosen was a 75bhp 1,100cc Climax FWA, similar to that used in the Lewis Special. Chapman was obviously designing the prototype as a sure-fire winner; what better advertisement for a new model, even if the production versions offered for sale were to be constructed to a rather more modest specification? Lewis's car went down in the Lotus records as being chassis number 400, although Lewis recalls that there was no chassis plate.

Edward Lewis took delivery of his new car in time for the Brighton Speed Trials of September 1957. He had a few problems getting to grips with the powerful little machine and in the wet on his first run spun and very nearly ended up in the sea. However, he recovered on his next attempt and recorded a time of 29.72 seconds to win his class. Lewis took the car to Prescott next day where he enjoyed success again, winning the 1,100cc sports car class by a whisker from a similarly powered Eleven. Very soon, even before the Seven had been officially announced, Lotus engineering were receiving enquiries about the new 'mystery' model which Lewis always took the trouble to prepare immaculately.

Lewis was to compete with the car for two seasons, fitting it with a 1,500cc Climax engine in 1958. Eventually he sold it to a Typhoo Tea travelling salesman, less engine, for £900; a great deal more than he would ever have got for the Edward Lewis special. His wisdom in agreeing to Chapman's proposal of a swap was proven.

Customers who wanted to buy production versions of the Seven prototype had to wait, because the exact specification of

the production version was still not complete. Naturally the cost of the production Seven had to be kept as low as possible, so the de Dion rear end as standard was out of the question. So were disc brakes and a Climax engine. Colin Chapman had been back to his drawing board to draw up a scheme for a live-axled Seven with drum brakes and Ford sidevalve engine but still with the Twelve front suspension. He presented it to draughtsman Ian Jones to knock into shape.

Jones duly accomplished this, taking just a week to finish it. However, even before he had produced the final version of the

drawing, Progress Chassis were at work producing the chassis. Outline plans had been sent to them at an early stage simply so they could get on with cutting tubes and setting up a jig because the first car was intended to be ready for the Earls Court Motor Show and that was little more than two months away.

John Teychenne and his foreman Frank Coltman at Progress Chassis were sufficiently-tuned in to what Lotus wanted to be able to work on this basis. As Ian Jones recalls, 'They were so clued up that you could just draw a detail with no diameter or what have you; you could just put a picture on a drawing board

18

The production specification Seven at last. Colin Chapman stands by the new model at the time of its unveiling which coincided with the 1957 Motor Show although the car was not displayed at Earls Court.

and they would give you back something that worked, because they knew enough.' Part way through construction, the finished drawing was ready and sent to Progress and within a short time the completed chassis was delivered back to Hornsey where it was panelled in aluminium by Williams and Pritchard and then carried into the adjacent Lotus workshop to be built up.

However, there simply wasn't enough time before the Earls Court Motor Show to get the Seven finished. The bulk of the effort at Hornsey had gone into getting the Lotus Elite ready in time and sure enough this sleek GT was the star of the 1957 Show. The offical launch of the Seven was a much lower-key affair. In the Motor Show issue of *The Autocar*, it was recorded that 'Lotus Engineering have introduced the Mark 7 although, they have been unable to display it at Earls Court. However, an example is available for inspection at the Lotus engineering Works, 7 Tottenham Lane, Hornsey, London N8.'

CHAPTER 3

Into production

The Seven Series 1 1957-1960

The first production Lotus Seven was offered complete and ready to go at a basic price of £1,036 including purchase tax. But in the kit form in which Chapman wanted to sell most cars, the total was a very attractive £536 because no purchase tax was levied. To comply with the laws relating to home-assembled cars, the chassis and engine were supplied by different companies, Lotus Engineering and Lotus Engines, both with the same business address, of course!

The Seven may have been the spiritual successor to the Mark 6 in being, 'the simplest, most basic, lightest, highest performance little car that we could come up with for two people at minimum cost,' to use Chapman's own words, but it was closer in execution to the Eleven. The Mark 6 had had a spaceframe chassis based around two larger bottom rails but the Seven had a uniform 18swg 1in tubular spaceframe with secondary tubes of ¾in.

The Seven's floor and propshaft tunnel were designed to be stressed and were riveted in position for extra strength. The aluminium cladding was also rivetted to the frame to increase its already impressive stiffness. Like the Mark 6, the Seven had no doors, but the sides of the car were sufficiently low for stepping in and out to be easy. An aluminium bonnet was held in place by over-centre clips and the nose cone located by four Dzus fasteners, lifting away to expose the radiator and chassis front. The mudguards were rigidly mounted to the car on brackets provided on the bottom and top chassis rails. The mudguards didn't turn with the steering and only covered the wheels fully in the straight-ahead position; cornering in the wet would be a very damp business for Seven owners.

Front suspension on the production Seven was borrowed from the Twelve, as on Lewis's prototype car. This clever and effective system employed twin wishbones, with the front link of the upper wishbone formed by the anti-roll bar which ran across the front of the chassis to which it was connected by aluminium yokes. In extreme racing conditions this arrangement was not ideal as it did allow compliance in the upper wishbone, but being compact, simple and efficient, it was ideal for the Seven. Even the fact that it offered no control over camber angle wasn't too much of a problem. At each side a coil spring and Armstrong telescopic damper unit was mounted between the base of the hub assembly and the top rail of the chassis.

Colin Chapman selected a live rear axle for the Seven. This was a BMC unit from the Nash Metropolitan as used on the 'Club' version of the Eleven. It was located by twin trailing arms with lateral location achieved by a link between the offside end of the axle and the chassis at the rear of the transmission tunnel. The upper radius arms kept the distinctive curved shape of those on the Eleven. As at the front, the rear axle had coil spring and damper units. The normal ratio of the final drive was 4.8:1 but numerous alternatives were available to meet all eventualities.

The brakes were hydraulically operated Ford drums, 9in at the front and 8in at the rear, while an ingenious location was devised for the handbrake which was hidden under the scuttle at the passenger side, mounted horizontally. This was fine in terms of keeping the lever out of the way but at the expense of making it very awkward to reach, especially with a passenger in place.

Colin Chapman was not an enthusiast for steering boxes as the steering quality they gave was not as precise and accurate as a rack-and-pinion system. But in the interests of keeping costs low, a Burman box was selected for the Seven. This was mounted behind the front wheel line and connected to the steering wheel by a column with two universal joints.

Ford power had proved very successful in the Mark 6 and

1,172cc engines as used in the Ford 100E were cheap and plentiful. Moreover, cars so equipped were eligible for the very popular 1172 Formula, run by the 750 Motor club. So this humble sidevalve engine, as used in the majority of Mark 6s, was

Colin Chapman's LOTUS SEVEN

HE designed it — YOU build it

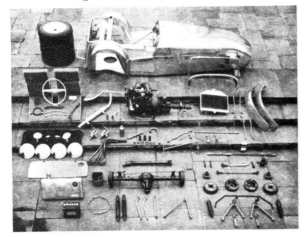

do it YOURSELF — at home
no special tools — only 60 hours work
all new parts — write for prices

LOTUS Engineering Co. Ltd. 7 TOTTENHAM LANE · HORNSEY LONDON N.8 · TEL: FITzroy 1777

The

LOTUS SEVEN

With a multi-tubular space frame based on that of the Le Mans-winning Lotus Eleven, and a simple, practical body reminiscent of the successful Lotus Mk. VI, the new Lotus Seven is an economically priced two-seat sports car for the man who means to enjoy his motoring to the full. Spartan in appearance, and hence light, the Seven nevertheless possesses all the most modern adjuncts to high performance ; an extremely rigid frame, Lotus L2 Type wishbone front suspension, live rear axle located by twin radius arms and "A" bracket, drum brakes and using the Ford 100E engine and gearbox. The low centre of gravity and a high degree of stability make the Lotus Seven an exceptional design. Using a high proportion of easily obtained production components, and straightforward in design, the Seven is also an ideal vehicle for the man who would like to build his own car.

LOTUS ENGINEERING CO., LTD.

TOTTENHAM LANE, HORNSEY, LONDON, N.8   Tel: MOUntview 8353

Two of the earliest advertisements for the Lotus Seven used in the magazine *Sports Car and Lotus Owner*. The copy extols the car's virtues and emphasizes the ease of construction from the complete kit of parts that cost £536. Those customers who did place orders in late 1957 were in for a wait though, as deliveries did not start properly until the spring of 1958.

adopted as standard for the Seven. It was mated with the normal Ford three-speed gearbox which has given a rudimentary but effective remote control gear linkage. Twin SU carburettors, a 'special' exhaust manifold and Buckler close-ratio gears all appeared on the options list. Whichever exhaust manifold was chosen, the main exhaust pipe ran along the left-hand side of the car and vented a short way in front of the rear tyre.

The fittings in the new car were few and far between. Non-adjustable 'seats' comprised a single piece foam-filled back section and two bases which laid directly on the floor. Chapman considered his own dimensions to be typical of the 'average' motorist and he built his cars accordingly; pity those Lotus owners who were taller or shorter than his 5ft 9in.

The Seven's seats were trimmed in red Vynide with white piping. This red matched the red covering on the inner side panels and dashboard, both of which were of metal with the Vynide stretched over and glued. There was no floor covering and no side protection and the tonneau cover and hood were optional extras. On early Sevens the dashboard was held in place by Dzus fasteners but these were later replaced by screws.

Instrumentation was fairly basic. The Mark 6 had a raised section on the dashboard which allowed all the instruments to be grouped in front of the driver. However, the Seven had a flat-top dash which allowed less space for instruments so a small, 3in speedo was chosen and mounted in front of the driver. On either side of the speedo were an oil pressure gauge and a water temperature gauge while the ammeter was banished to the passenger side.

There was no fuel gauge or tachometer. Customers could fit their own tacho if they wished, while fuel checks were designed to be carried out by removing the fuel cap in the 'boot' and peering inside the tank. The tank was a Williams and Pritchard aluminium fabrication with a 7-gallon capacity. It was held in place by elastic ropes and Chapman must have been fairly sure that it was securely fixed because he located the battery right next door on a little perch welded to the chassis.

A quickly detachable full-width screen was standard on the Seven but there was no provision for integral wipers. However, an add-on wiper system driven from a motor mounted at the screen top could be fitted. The Seven's headlighting system left

FVV 877 with rather makeshift number-plate as tested by *The Autocar* in November 1957. Changes from its first appearance included a different exhaust system and the fitting of rudimentary windscreen wipers.

Weather protection on the new Lotus ran to the extent of a hood although as revealed in this shot, its quality was poor and the fit indifferent. Getting in and out of the car with the hood up was something of a challenge.

The nosecone of Ford-powered S1 Sevens had a hole through which protruded the cap of the brass radiator. Note the vintage style headlamps, only one of which operated on dipped beam. The front suspension design in which the front link of the upper wishbone was formed by an anti-roll bar was borrowed from the Twelve single seater.

something to be desired, comprising two Lucas units, operating on the antiquated system whereby the offside light went out completely on dipped beam. A small chrome sidelight sat atop each mudguard. At the rear, single lenses doubled as brake and rear lights. There were no indicators.

Fitted with 15in Ford wheels with shiny hub caps, the very first production Seven was running by October 1957. It had chassis number 401 and was registered FVV 877, or more accurately fitted with registration plates bearing that number. They had come from the Edward Lewis special which had been sold abroad.

Once shakedown tests were complete and several thousand test miles had been completed, FVV 877 was subjected to the ultimate test; ordeal by motoring magazine. In November 1957 it

was collected by *The Autocar* for the very first road test.

Painted pale yellow, FVV cut quite a dash with its red trim and optional hood. It was kitted out with the optional tonneau cover and spare wheel plus full tool kit, while the engine had the performance extras of twin carbs and a special manifold.

Road testers in the late 1950s were less prone to scatter superlatives than their modern counterparts, but the Seven went down very well with what was then the country's most influential motoring journal. 'One soon forgets minor discomforts in the exhilaration of its performance...An outstanding feature of the car is the road-holding and general stability... Ideal road and race car,' are just three of their conclusions.

When *The Motor* borrowed FVV some weeks later, that magazine's testers were similarly enthusiastic about the new little

The Seven's cockpit was hardly spacious, but adequate for two sporting motorists with minimal luggage. Instrumentation comprised a speedometer, plus gauges for oil pressure, water temperature and amps. Interior trim was in standard red Vynide with white piping. The three-speed Ford gearbox was equipped with a straightforward remote control lever.

sports car. They managed to make it reach 80.4mph and top 60mph in 16.2 seconds, improvements over *The Autocar's* figures (Appendix B) that suggest that Mike Costin may have spent a little time making the engine run more sweetly.

The queue of customers for Sevens was getting longer towards the end of 1957 but none of them actually took delivery of a car. The workshop at Hornsey was bursting at the seams and neither the space nor the manpower was available to build Sevens. Not until early 1958 did things really get going.

The first person to buy a production Seven was 20-year old Brian Luff who soon afterwards came to work for Lotus as a design draughtsman. Luff had in fact placed an order for one of the last batch of Mark 6s built up from spare chassis in 1956, but the car never arrived. Eventually he went back to see smooth-talking salesman Colin Bennet who persuaded him to wait instead for one of the new Sevens, even though at that time he couldn't tell him precisely what it was going to look like! Luff: 'A couple of months after deciding to have the Seven, I called in again to see Bennet and he told me that the car would be ready for collection the next Saturday. I duly turned up and nobody knew anything about it.'

This carried on for several weeks until eventually Luff was able to collect his chassis. But only the chassis! Of the remainder of the car there was no sign. Eventually more bits and pieces were forthcoming, but it took a full four months before Stores Manager John Standen was able to come up with sufficient parts for the car to be completed. Luff recalls that he had so much time to spare that he polished the outside of the engine. It was the spring of 1958 before this car took to the road, complete with optional Aquaplane aluminium alloy cylinder head. Luff also fitted an aluminium flywheel, and special pistons that cost 56 shillings each; a fortune in those days.

Rear end details of FVV 877 showing the Nash Metropolitan axle located by twin radius arms. Note the extensive riveting of the transmission tunnel. The hood sticks, tool wrap and spare wheel all visible here were optional extras.

A recent shot of an S1 Seven in the course of restoration showing the diagonal link that provides lateral location for the axle. Note the curvature of the upper radius arm, a hangover from the de Dion rear suspension. The rear undertray was dropped on later Sevens.

FVV 877 with the nosecone removed to reveal the front suspension complete with integral anti-roll bar. The hefty brass radiator is a distinctive S1 Seven feature. This car was fitted with the standard 1,172cc Ford sidevalve engine but equipped with the option of twin carburettors. Throttle actuation was via a solid rod that ran from the pedal across the bulkhead straight to the carbs. This led to very jerky operation for those with insensitive feet.

Registered UOW 429, Luff's car was to become quite famous as it was featured on the first Lotus Seven brochure. Peter Warr, who today runs Team Lotus, took over as Sales Manager in mid 1959 and one of the tasks he set himself was to produce a proper brochure for the Seven as production was at last getting going properly. However, there was no works-owned Ford-powered car available at that time as the first production example had been sold off some time previously. Warr therefore persuaded Brian Luff to part with his car for the brochure photo session. Warr soon broke the news to Luff that he needed to keep the car longer than just the one day. He wanted it for display at the first London DIY Show. If Luff agreed to this he'd be provided with a spare wheel for his car. To save money Luff had opted not to have this optional £11 17s 6d extra, so he agreed. The car was duly exhibited at Olympia and then returned to Luff, complete with spare wheel. Only later did Luff discover that the spare wheel

What may be considered the first real 'customer' Seven was UOW 429 which was ordered by Brian Luff and registered in early 1958. Luff built up the car with great care; he had time to do this as missing kit parts took so long to arrive!

Luff's car was fitted with an Aquaplane cylinder head, aluminium flywheel and special pistons so not only was it one of the best looking Sevens but it was also one of the fastest at the time.

At a loss for a car to feature in Seven advertising and in the first brochure, Sales Manager Peter Warr borrowed Luff's car for a photographic session and subsequent display at the Olympia DIY Exhibition for which Luff was 'paid' with a new spare wheel which he later discovered didn't fit!

didn't fit; it was from a Ford Consul and was the wrong size!

Lotus Engineering sold their cars direct to the public at that time. However, those customers who were lucky enough to receive a letter from Mrs Hazel Chapman telling them that their Lotus Replica kit was ready for collection still had quite a way to go before they were mobile. For their £536 they received a bare aluminium-panelled chassis unit already fitted with rear wings, wiring loom, brake pipes, master cylinder, regulator and solenoid. The dashboard was fitted out with all instrumentation with the notable exception of the speedometer, due to a quirk of home assembly regulations. The engine had been test-fitted although it came as a separate assembly, ready connected to the gearbox and with the clutch in place. The kit was designed to be carted away in a small van or on the roof of a saloon car.

Various boxes and cloth bags accompanied the kit and contained all the smaller components, sub-assemblies and fastenings. The axle was ready 'dressed' with the appropriate brackets welded in place and came complete with brake drums and handbrake linkage. Assemblies such as the coil spring and damper units which required a special spring compressor for assembly were supplied complete.

With the advent of the Seven, Lotus took the kit car concept into the next era. No longer would the buyer have to rush around from supplier to supplier trying to locate bits which he would then have to modify with a hacksaw or welding torch. Instead, armed with an average tool kit, a pair of trestles and a hoist, plus maybe a friend or two, he would find that a Seven could be screwed together in a week's spare time or maybe even less. The 12-hour build time that Lotus claimed in advertisements was maybe a little optimistic.

Even at this early stage, Inland Revenue inspectors showed a keen interest in the Seven, just waiting for Lotus to overstep the mark and offer a car that was too fully assembled. Eventually a friendly rapport was struck up with the inspectors, although quite what a kit car manufacturer could or could not do was never committed to paper; the whole procedure was based on a series of 'friendly chats'.

One thing Lotus certainly could not do was supply building instructions with the kit. That was overcome in two main ways. The first was to supply a journalist with a kit, the assembly of which he described in great detail in *Sports Car and Lotus Owner*. The second method adopted some years later was to include a chapter in the owner's manual dealing with the repair of a Seven

This is what the recipient of a Lotus Seven kit was confronted with. The basic chassis unit was wired and plumbed but all the ancillaries and sub-assemblies came separately. It was claimed that no special tools were needed to build up the car. This chassis had already been painted; normally it arrived in bare aluminium.

following a major accident. Naturally this involved a complete strip down and rebuild...

When it came to ease of assembly, some buyers were luckier than others. The cramped conditions at Hornsey in which storeman John Standen operated were not ideal for making sure that every kit had exactly the right quota of bits and pieces, so maybe he should be forgiven for the occasional lapse.

John Derisley bought his first Seven in early 1958 and had to make half a dozen trips back to Hornsey to round up all the missing bits and hand back some items that were surplus to requirements. Even then he was left without any wheel nuts. 'I complained on the telephone about the wheel nuts,' he recalls, 'and all of a sudden about eight sets arrived, all in separate packages!'

A handful of very early Sevens were supplied with Burman steering boxes but Colin Chapman was still not happy with the system and the chassis was modified to accommodate a modified Morris Minor steering rack. This was mounted upside down, on brackets welded to the chassis, but the location remained behind the wheel line. It gave the steering much more feel and overcame a vagueness in the straight-ahead position about which various owners and testers had complained. The first Seven to be fitted with rack-and-pinion steering was none other than FVV 877, which, as well as being the road test car, was used as a test bed for new ideas. Brian Luff's car was also recalled to have the box replaced by a rack-and-pinion and all production cars thereafter were so fitted.

By May 1958, the factory decided that the time had come to part with FVV and this hardworking little car was taken to bits and offered for sale as a used kit. The enthusiastic buyer was

An historic moment captured by Warren King as he prepares to leave the Hornsey factory with the first production Seven on the roof of his Riley. Having done service as a development and road test car, FVV 877 was sold to King as a second-hand kit that he built up and re-registered 3 LVX.

Warren King, an expatriate Australian who had come to the UK looking for a job involved with cars. He was to find a job – at Lotus – a year later, but in the meantime he busied himself working in a cardboard box factory and building up his new acquisition. Being something of a perfectionist, King took his time; the finished car was assembled beautifully and registered 3 LVX.

Colin Chapman had hoped to have production of Elites in full swing by 1958 but production difficulties meant that this just didn't happen. So the Seven took on a more important role than had been planned for it, and it became a good money-spinner for Lotus Engineering. Whenever there was a space in the workshop a Seven kit would start springing up. Chapman was later to pay tribute to the Seven in this respect: 'It was the Seven and the sports cars that made Lotus; all the profit that they brought in we squandered on trying to build the Elite which was a complete disaster because we lost so much money on each car...It was five years before the road cars made any money.'

Very nearly all the early Sevens left Hornsey with Ford 100E engines, but Colin Chapman hoped to be able to sell Sevens with more powerful engines for use in racing categories other than the 1172 Formula. And what more suitable engine than the 1,098cc Coventry Climax of the type fitted to Edward Lewis's prototype car? This popular small engine was made of light alloy and produced a healthy 75bhp at 6,250rpm when fitted with twin SU carburettors and a four-branch exhaust manifold.

Two Climax-engined Sevens had already been produced in addition to Lewis's car. The first of these was destined for Jack Richards, had chassis number 404 and was registered TBY 484. Richards was Competition Secretary of Club Lotus and his car was built up at the factory to the highest concours standards. This car, like Lewis's, had a de Dion axle and disc brakes all

Jack Richards, Competition Secretary of Club Lotus, bought an early Seven built to a specification similar to Edward Lewis's car, with Climax engine, de Dion rear suspension and disc brakes. Tested by *Sports Car and Lotus Owner* in April 1958 it was described as a 'one in a million sports car'. It was beautifully prepared with extensive chroming and polishing of the 80bhp Climax engine. Top speed of this formidable little car was above the 100mph mark. The front suspension was standard S1 Seven, but with disc brakes. The discs at the rear were mounted inboard.

A classic pair. The innovative glassfibre monocoque Lotus Elite was introduced at the same time as the Seven. The Seven seen here is the first production Super Seven, registered 7 TMT. This 1,100cc Coventry Climax-engined car was raced by Graham Hill at the 1958 Boxing Day Brands Hatch meeting, then became the factory demonstrator before being bought and used for 30,000 road miles by Peter Warr, one-time boss of Lotus Components and nowadays Director of Team Lotus.

round. The second car to this advanced specification was built some time later and sold to Graham Warner who ran the well-known Chequered Flag car dealership and had a motor racing team of the same name.

A production Seven with a de Dion axle and disc brakes would have had a very limited market because of the high cost, so Chapman simply offered the standard car with a Climax engine, plus matched gearbox and a few other sporty mods. The Climax-engined Seven was offered in Lotus advertisements as early as February 1958 but the first production 'Super Seven', as the model was christened, was not built until December 1958. It was given a baptism of fire, being raced by Graham Hill at Brands Hatch on Boxing Day. The race was wet and Hill beat all the streamlined cars to score a headline-making victory that got the new model off on the right foot.

The Ford-powered cars had the Ford three-speed gearbox as standard, but this unit was unsuitable for such a sporty engine as the Climax, so Mike Costin, who oversaw the development department, chose instead the four-speed unit of the Austin A30 and fitted it with close-ratio gears. A thick aluminium sandwich

plate was fitted to mate the engine and gearbox.

The first Super Seven was built in the time-honoured Lotus manner. A Seven chassis was brought in to the workshop and the engine/gearbox unit hoisted roughly into place. Measurements were taken and with deft use of hacksaw and welding torch, both engine and gearbox mountings were fabricated. Peter Warr recalls that the necessary adjustments to the chassis tubes to accommodate the new gearbox were marked with chalk but while the chassis was sitting out in the yard, a sudden rainstorm washed all the chalk away and the whole operation had to be repeated!

Apart from the engine and gearbox, this upmarket version of the Seven was very similar to the basic car. The final drive was made a little longer at 4.55:1 to allow for the greater speed potential. Other small differences included the fitting of a sporty three-spoke leather rimmed steering wheel to replace the normal two-spoke plastic affair. Also, a tachometer became standard in place of the speedometer. 15in wire wheels also became standard with a spare wheel included in the basic price of £700 for the kit. This made the Climax-powered Seven a little under £120 more expensive than the basic car. Playing on the words 'souped-up'

A view of the Seven production area at the Cheshunt factory in late 1959, not long after the move from Hornsey. Note the aluminium wings and nosecone of these S1 Sevens under construction.

the new version was officially listed as the 'Super Seven' and the basic model designated Seven F to differentiate it from its bigger brother.

The extra 35bhp of the Super Seven made all the difference in the world. Top speed was boosted to more than 100mph with 60mph reached in 9.2 seconds and superb tractability throughout the speed range. Such impressive performance notwithstanding, the Super Seven still managed 30 miles on a gallon of fuel. As a combined road car and competition car the Super Seven was unrivalled.

The first Super Seven was registered 7 TMT and after being raced by Graham Hill, became the works demonstrator for a while. It was road tested by John Bolster for *Autosport* and David Phipps for *Sports Car and Lotus Owner*. Phipps tested the car at night in a snowstorm and his report didn't include any performance figures. Bolster, on the other hand, was luckier with the weather and managed 104.6mph, finding the car tremendously exciting and tractable. He also found that: 'A large man in a leather coat may enter the Super Seven without too much difficulty; getting out requires a good deal more effort.'

7 TMT was used as the demonstrator for several months and then bought for £750 by Sales Manager Peter Warr as his personal car. He kept it for two years and covered 30,000 road and race miles with almost total reliability. One of his lasting memories of the bright red car with its chromed exhaust and wire wheels was encountering a policeman on his regular commuting journey between Farningham and the Lotus factory. 'I came along a 40mph stretch one night, just on 40mph, and picked up a policeman in my rear-view mirror. We left the restricted area and came to some traffic lights. He pulled up alongside on his big Triumph, lifted up his goggles and leant over. All he said was, "Nice car, what'll she do?" I said, "It's not very quick, 100mph or so." Then he said, "Come on, I'll give you a go," and that was the first and only time I've ever entered into a sporting venture with a cop. We had the most almighty drag race from the lights and I only just beat him because I could leave my braking later at the next roundabout! That was the sort of car it was; attracted attention wherever you went.'

As Colin Chapman had intended, the majority of Sevens did not deviate from the standard specifications. However, the fact that the Eleven's de Dion suspension would fit in the Seven's chassis with very little modification led some customers to improve their cars in this way. Similarly, the adjustable top link front suspension of the Fifteen could be adapted for the Seven and at least one car survives as proof that this system was tried by some owners.

Approximately 100 Sevens were built in 1958; most Ford powered but with a sprinkling of Climax-powered cars for the better-off customers. The Lotus star was still very much in the ascendant at the time with the marque enjoying success after success at every level of motor sport. The Eleven was still going strong, but the Hornsey factory was also turning out the Fifteen sports racer and the Sixteen single seater, while the rear-engined Eighteen was waiting in the wings. At long last a new office building and stores had been built at Hornsey. Williams and Pritchard moved from the Hornsey site to a new building in Edmonton next door to the Progress Chassis Co who had outgrown their unsuitable Hornsey premises some time

previously. However, space for the 20-strong Lotus Engineering workforce was still ridiculously cramped. Development of the time-consuming Elite project had been moved out to a rented workshop in Edmonton. It was clear that Lotus couldn't carry on much longer the way things were, and already Colin Chapman was looking for new premises.

The search led further north from London to a Development Area in Cheshunt and a patch of land on an industrial park. Plans were lodged for two adjacent factory buildings with a roadway between. However, there was no way that the new premises would be ready before the spring of 1959, so the team at Hornsey had to be patient.

The standard working week at Hornsey was 47 hours including a compulsory Saturday morning. 'We were lucky if we got away with twice that,' recalls Peter Brand, who joined Lotus as a fitter in May 1959. 'It was a case of keep going until the work's finished and the last man out throws the keys through the letter box.' On only his second day at Hornsey, Brand worked right through to 4 o'clock the next morning. He then bicycled home, grabbed a few hours sleep and was back at 8am to start again! 'People didn't

Exterior of the Lotus Components factory at Cheshunt. Clearly visible is the loading door from which Sevens, built on the upper floor, had to be lowered by winch to ground level.

mind giving that level of commitment,' he says. 'You had the satisfaction of seeing a car you'd built winning a race the next Saturday.' Soon after starting work at Hornsey, Peter Brand began building Sevens, a job he was to continue for almost seven years.

During May 1959, the Cheshunt factory was far enough advanced for production of the Elite to be moved there. To coincide with the move, Colin Chapman decided to reorganize his company. Powerful personality that he was, he believed that the most efficient way for the company to be run was to break it down into smaller units, each with its own boss. Such an

arrangement also meant that Chapman could spend time away with Team Lotus in the knowledge that business would carry on without him. In the new structure, Chapman was to maintain overall control but each manager could run his group as he saw fit. Accordingly, the arrangement that had prevailed at Hornsey with Lotus Engineering, Racing Engines and Team Lotus, was adjusted to become Lotus Cars, who would build the Elite, Team Lotus, who would run the works racing team, Lotus Components who would build the Seven and all the customer racing cars, and then finally Lotus Developments who were responsible for engineering new models and specification changes. Lotus Service was established as a subsidiary of Lotus Cars. Employees at Hornsey were notified of the company reorganization and offered jobs at the new factory along with a pay rise from 4s 10d per hour to 5s 1d if they chose to move; very nearly all of them did.

The entire Lotus operation was successfully installed in the new factory by June 1959, although the official opening ceremony wasn't held until October. One of the first new employees engaged at Cheshunt was none other than Warren King, who had bought the first production Seven the previous year. He joined as an accounts clerk and commuted to Cheshunt in his trusty Seven.

From the beginning, Lotus had sold cars direct from the factory, but Colin Chapman appreciated that with the numbers of vehicles he was hoping to shift after the move to Cheshunt it simply wasn't realistic to continue in this way. He needed a proper sales network and set about negotiating with various dealers round the UK who would become official 'Lotus Centres'.

At Cheshunt, newly-established Lotus Components was run by long-serving Nobby Clarke who had been one of the original 'Hornsey Volunteers'. He had Roy Badcock as his foreman and the two set about organizing their new department. An assembly area was established on the ground floor and the stores kept on a mezzanine level above. Construction of racing cars took priority at this stage and production of Sevens wasn't able to get into full swing until the autumn of 1959.

Peter Brand was assigned to building the first of the Cheshunt Sevens and he began work in the general Components workshop which was in the right-hand of the two Cheshunt factories. A waiting list for the Sevens had built up by that time after the lull in production, so it seemed obvious to establish a special area specifically for the assembly of Seven kits. The sense of this was that parts and tools could be kept near at hand and the whole assembly process made better organized and speeded up.

Consequently, planning permission was sought to convert the mezzanine storeroom into a workshop. The floor was strengthened and the area fitted out with the necessary equipment. All the bits and pieces needed to build Sevens were moved up there in October 1959. The only problem with this upstairs arrangement was getting the finished kits and the occasional complete car down to the ground. This was solved using the winch and delivery hatch at the front of the building. A cradle was constructed that attached to the four corners of the car and, using this and the winch, Sevens could be gently lowered.

With 1960 just around the corner, Colin Chapman was keen to tap the export potential of his cars. The American market looked particularly fruitful and the Seven featured in these plans. Several Sevens had already found their way to the United States but it was clear that a Seven produced specifically for that market place stood an even better chance of success. There were problems though, because American buyers seemed to want a higher level of trim than the UK Seven offered. Proper windscreen wipers would be needed for a start and a better lighting system was essential, as were turn indicators.

The Seven's cycle wings presented a particular problem as USA legislation didn't permit them. Colin Chapman had produced drawings of flared wings for the Seven as early as 1957, both with the American market in mind, and also with the aim of generally increasing driver protection in the Seven. Using Chapman's drawings, Williams and Pritchard built two or three sets of flared wings in aluminium for the first American spec Seven. When it came to putting the wings into full production the decision was made to use glassfibre, a material that had much less 'black art' associated with it than two years previously.

American buyers were not too enthusiastic about the 100E sidevalve engine. The sweet-revving overhead-valve BMC A-series engine of the Morris Minor and Austin-Healey Sprite impressed them much more. With its normal four-speed gearbox, this engine was ideal for the Seven, so it was chosen to power the Seven America, having already been added to the list of engines available for the Seven at home. In twin SU carburettor form, the A-series unit produced 40bhp at 5,000rpm and gave a top speed of around 85mph with acceleration to 60mph in 14 seconds.

Peter Brand assembled the prototype Seven America in late 1959. This car was right-hand drive and painted bright red. It had proper windscreen wipers driven from a motor mounted under the scuttle, a manually-switched electric fan was squeezed into the front of the engine bay and sealed-beam headlights replaced the usual tiny lamps. The Seven America even had carpets and a full-length tonneau from which the 'doors' could be clipped in separately. The instrumentation was better too, with a tachometer and speedometer as standard, the latter located right

In late 1959, the BMC A-series engine of the Austin A35 or Austin-Healey Sprite was added to the list of options for the Seven with the USA market particularly in mind. This is the lower-powered single carb unit although the majority had twin SUs fitted. Fitting this engine had the added benefit of allowing the use of the four-speed BMC gearbox.

Flared wings were seen on a Seven for the first time with the advent of the Seven America, seen here on display at a car show in Detroit in early 1960. The car was still right-hand drive but had improved lights, better instrumentation and standard windscreen wipers.

over on the passenger side of the dashboard. Before the prototype was despatched to the States it went on display at the second London DIY Show.

While Lotus Components continued building the Series 1 in its various forms during the first half of 1960, Mike Costin's Development department had been finding time in a frantic schedule to work on Colin Chapman's idea for a revised version of the Seven. A Seven for the 1960s.

CHAPTER 4

A Seven for the 1960s

The Seven Series 2 1960-1968

The Series 1 Seven did its job. During 1958 and 1959 it filled in the gaps in production and provided vital income at a time when the company as a whole was still virtually awash with the crippling expense of building the Elite. By 1960 the Seven was a vital part of Lotus Components' activities and already almost 250 units had been built. However, there was potential for greater numbers to be built and for more money to be made.

The Seven had not been making as much money as it could, mainly because it was taking too long to build. Around 60 hours was the average time it took the fitters assigned to the task to construct a Seven kit; not a complete car mind, just a kit. The time was being lost in persuading bits and pieces to fit. There simply wasn't sufficient consistency in the dimensions to which the chassis was made.

There was also the problem that the chassis were expensive to buy in. If the design could be simplified, the cost would be reduced. After discussing it with Progress Chassis, Colin Chapman therefore set about removing from the original design all the tubes he could, relying on the riveted aluminium skin to maintain chassis stiffness. Riveting in the inner body panels and dashboard also helped compensate for the loss of tubes.

The original drawing by Ian Jones for what became known as the Series 2 Seven is dated as early as November 16, 1959 but the model wasn't listed until June 1960. The new version differed from the first Seven in several respects apart from the number of chassis tubes. The undertray of the Series 1 Seven had extended beneath the engine compartment and under the boot but for the Series 2, it was foreshortened. At the front it now stopped at the bulkhead and at the rear it ended at the seat back. The problem with the S1 undertray was that it was a tight fit round the sump and quite often had to be trimmed to suit. The panel was unsupported so the trimmed edge then had to be wired and rolled to give it some strength. Peter Brand recalls often spending hours with a dolly and planishing hammer working on this undertray. Discontinuing the undertray at the rear prevented mud collecting and allowed easier access to the axle.

Another change Peter Brand was glad to see was the redesign of the petrol tank. The capacity was increased and it was made in steel rather than aluminium for the first time. At last it was properly located with steel straps rather than elastic ropes. At the same time, the battery was moved from next to the tank to perch on the bulkhead in the engine compartment. The inner side trim panels and dashboard of the S2 were made of 'skin plate', metal with Vynide ready bonded to it. This would save time stretching and gluing aluminium and Vynide together. On the S1, the dash panel fitted flush to the chassis tubes, but the riveted dash of the S2 wrapped round the bottom tube and left no sharp edge.

Chassis tubes that disappeared with the advent of the S2 included the diagonals in the sides of the engine bay plus the two diagonals in the cockpit sides. Also the amount of tube used in the seat back was reduced and the steel hoop at the rear of the transmission tunnel dropped. These particular changes at the rear of the chassis were associated with the introduction of an A-frame to locate the rear axle. This replaced the semi A-frame of the Series 1: that had fed its stresses to the chassis just behind the seat and consequently the structure needed triangulating in that area on the earlier car.

The A-frame was not a Chapman invention but on the Seven it

The A-frame method of locating the rear axle as applied to the S2 Seven by Colin Chapman. The disadvantage of the system was that high loads were fed into the axle casing. Without reinforcement the casing tended to distort and crack.

was employed in an economical and effective way. It was combined with a single straight radius arm at each side to provide an excellently located axle at the expense of feeding stresses into the axle casing. These forces were magnified by the fact that the centre of the A-frame was located on a rubber-bushed bracket welded to the bottom of the axle. Most previous examples of the A-frame system had been connected to the top of the axle which gave the axle casing an easier life. However, adopting a similar system on the Seven would have made the roll centres too high for good handling. Besides which, Chapman calculated that with the range of engines he had in mind for the Seven, the axle could cope with the stresses involved.

Triumph introduced the innovative Herald range in 1959 and Lotus were quick to recognize that the front suspension uprights and the steering rack were ideal for the Series 2 Seven. The pitch circle diameter (PCD) of the new front hubs was different from those of the Series 1 which were of Hillman origin. To keep the front and rear PCDs the same on the new car, the Nash Metropolitan axle was dispensed with and a comparable unit from a Standard Companion fitted instead, notwithstanding the fact that Standard had just dropped this model. Manufacturers were much more conscientious at providing obselete model support in those days and Lotus were confident that supplies would be available for the foreseeable future. The tubework around the axle was simplified and a tube added at each side running beneath the axle to compensate for the simplification. Also the spring/damper unit mounting points were moved to the top of the axle to share the radius arm attachments. To give the Series 2 Seven a more modern appearance, 13in wheels replaced the original 15in types and at the same time the option of wire wheels was deleted.

The change in make of the steering rack from Morris Minor to Triumph Herald provided an opportunity to reposition the rack in front of the wheel line. This improved the geometry of the column at the expense of losing the Ackerman effect that its previous rearward location had created. The Ackerman school of thought proposed that for better cornering, the inner wheel on the corner had to turn more than the outer. Placing the rack behind the wheel line created this condition since the steering arms converged towards the rear of the car.

However, the value of this Ackerman effect was questionable. Moreover, Lotus were anxious to create more foot space round the pedals by realigning the steering column which had hitherto passed through the pedal box. It was vital to drive an S1 Seven wearing narrow shoes or there was a real risk of getting your left foot jammed between the gearbox tunnel and the column. Moving the rack forward allowed the angle of the column to be reduced so it ran above the pedals and it also meant that the two universal joints formerly fitted in the column could be dispensed with. The column was linked straight to the rack with the use of a single splined clamp. The revised design allowed the use of a simpler rack mounting system which further reduced the number of chassis tubes needed in that area. Yet another benefit of this particular aspect of the redesign was that simpler engine mountings could be used without the need for the right-hand one to have a kink in it to clear the steering column.

The S2 Seven was already on the Lotus drawing boards when the S1 Seven America was conceived, so the flared wings which made that model so readily identifiable can really be regarded as an S2 feature. Initially customers could still have cycle wings if they wished but for the S2 Seven these were made in glassfibre rather than aluminium, as were the restyled rear wings and nosecone.

The advent of the S2 saw the use of a redesigned glassfibre nosecone and glassfibre wings. The grille was also revised. Although flared wings were fitted to the majority of S2s, cycle wings, also in glassfibre, continued to be available and were listed right up to 1965. The car in this shot has the later spec headlights; early S2s retained the basic Lucas system of the S1.

The use of glassfibre rather than hand-beaten aluminium was a major cost saving on the S2. The parts made in this material were easier to handle too, and the options of red, yellow or green self-pigmented glassfibre meant that the unpainted cars looked brighter and more exciting.

The new rear wings had a flatter and wider section that those of the S1, while the line of the nosecone was raised. This gave a more attractive frontal aspect which was complemented by the fitting of a neat chromed mesh grille to replace the rather heavy S1 design. Fixings for the nosecone remained Dzus fasteners, but the front fixing point was moved from mid-way down the nose to underneath, making the removal job quite a lot trickier. John Frayling, the man who executed the styling of the Elite, was responsible for the new nose and grille, as indeed he had been for the translation of the flared wings from aluminium to glassfibre.

Working in wood, plaster and lengths of welding wire, Frayling carved out the shapes of the new parts and built master moulds for them to be made in-house. The introduction of the new nosecone saw the moving of the coolant filler neck back into the engine bay with the introduction of a remote-filler radiator. Previously on most Sevens the radiator cap had protruded through the nosecone. Traditionalists bemoaned the passing of

Another version of 8843 AR, this time with flared wings, hood and optional side curtains which at last offered some elbow protection.

A basic S2 chassis photographed outside the Cheshunt factory. The glassfibre nose-cone is in place and the rear wings fitted. With the adoption of the A-frame method of rear axle location, the triangulation of tubes at the rear of the car was altered to suit the new load paths.

the S1's attractive brass-topped radiator.

With the commissioning of the first batch of S2 chassis, part of the contract for their construction was moved from the Progress Chassis Co to Universal Radiators of Northampton. Arch Motors of Tottenham, who were building racing chassis for Lotus, were approached to take over building the Seven's chassis but didn't have the spare capacity at that stage. Universal Radiators sent the completed frames to a firm called Alert Motors for panelling, from whence they were despatched to Cheshunt.

The prototype Series 2 Seven was also the first Seven to be made with left-hand drive. It was chassis number 999 and had an A-series Sprite engine fitted. While the 1,172cc Ford engine and three-speed gearbox were still listed as the base specification for the Seven, most early Series 2s were supplied with A-series power. Production S2 Sevens began at chassis number SB1000.

The advent of the new Ford Anglia 105E in 1959 provided Lotus with another engine to add to the range available, Caterham Cars' Works Manager, Peter Scott, having pioneered the fitting of this engine into the Seven. The 105E unit was a 997cc design with overhead valves. Converted to run on twin SU carburettors it made the right sort of noises and produced around 50bhp. Developments fitted a 105E engine to a Seven in late 1960 and that version became the 'Basic Seven', replacing both the

Very early S2 at Cheshunt. The car is shown with S1-type cycle wings and lights. S2 sales were flagging in late 1960 but the price cut to a basic £499 in January 1960 did the trick and the orders came pouring in.

Late 1961: a Super Seven in red with a 1,340cc Cosworth version of the Ford Classic 109E engine. This was a very fast Seven, capable of 103mph and accelerating to 60mph in just 7.6 seconds. Basic price for this version of the S2 was £599 in component form.

A popular powerplant for the early S2 was the 997cc Ford Anglia 105E engine fitted with SU twin carburettors. Note the location of the battery: on the S1 it had been next to the petrol tank in the boot but the S2 saw it mounted under the bonnet.

100E-powered version and the A-series car. It used a four-speed Anglia gearbox which had a Triumph remote control unit cleverly grafted on to it. Sevens with 105E engines were never particularly popular among the staff at Lotus Components who found the unit ran out of breath at 70mph. They looked back wistfully at test runs in Climax-powered cars over the 10-mile 'Mountain' road test circuit around Cheshunt and looked forward to the introduction of another Super Seven.

The Climax engine was dropped from the range for the S2 although it was included in the options listed in the first S2 advertisements. As part of the chassis redesign, the engine mountings had been revised and without chassis modifications the Climax unit wouldn't fit. Besides which it was expensive and there were other engines with plenty of tuning potential on the way from Ford. Mike Costin was still running the development department of Lotus at this time but had jointly established a

business with Keith Duckworth. Named Cosworth, this firm produced tuning components and specialized engines. Therefore it seemed only natural that Lotus should aim to fit Cosworth-tuned engines to the Super Seven instead of Climax units.

The S2 Seven was well received upon its introduction in June 1960. But not quite well enough. With the new Cheshunt workshop now building kits continuously, rather than using them to fill in, the end of the year saw Lotus in the unfortunate position of being unable to sell all the Sevens they were making. Chassis started piling up on nearby Panshangar airfield under makeshift polythene covers, while unsold kits had to be stored under cover in corners of the yard at Cheshunt. Something needed to be done. It was.

At the Racing Car Show in January 1961 Lotus announced that the price of the new 105E-engined Seven was to be £499 in kit form. This amounted to a saving of very nearly £100 on the old price for a basic Seven. Graham Nearn of Caterham Cars, one of the original Lotus Centres, was delighted when he heard the news as he knew he could sell many more cars. He wasn't quite so delighted when he then learned that his margin had been similarly pruned back to just £20 per car and that Lotus were going to start selling Sevens direct from the factory once more.

The price cut did the trick and launched something of a golden era for the Seven. Orders came pouring in. Some of the stockpiled chassis had been sitting for months and were in a terrible state but they were moved back inside the workshop to be cleaned up and fitted out. 'We never had any complaints,'recalls Peter Brand who, along with the other men assigned to building Sevens benefited from the introduction of a bonus scheme aimed at encouraging them to build faster!

As the workshop became better organized, so other aspects of Seven building were streamlined. By now the chassis dimensions and the panelling were much more consistent. A closer watch was being kept on the standards of bought-in components. For the first time a wiring loom was bought in complete. Previously the fitters had made their own looms using a complicated and time-

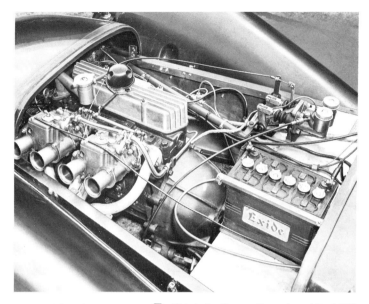

This is the Cosworth version of the 109E engine. The cast rocker cover was a distinctive Cosworth feature while the gasping twin Weber carburettors left onlookers in no doubt as to the engine's potency.

A-series engines were fitted to many early S2s before Ford engines became standard. In Sprite spec, with twin SU carburettors, the little engine was responsive, economical and easily tuneable.

Upstairs at Cheshunt with S2 production in full swing. Peter Brand, who was to be associated with Seven production for many years, tends to the nose of the car in the centre of the shot. Note the ubiquitous 8843 AR at the back of the workshop waiting to be fettled before going out for road test.

consuming wiring board. Suggestions for improvements often came from the Seven fitters themselves. Peter Brand recalls how after repeated requests to the development department, the anti-roll bar was delivered in a machined state, ready for fitting. 'Before that it took about two hours to fit properly,' he recalls. 'But then once it arrrived machined at the extra cost of a penny a unit, we could fit them up in ten minutes. In the end we got the construction time of the kit down to something like 12 hours.'

Templates were built to ensure that the distance between the windscreen pillars and the rear damper posts remained constant. Previously the screen had merely been offered up and drilled and bolted at a point where it 'looked right'. The variations that this introduced made hood fitting a very hit and miss affair. Jigs were also made for bending the hood sticks, but although the chassis were much more consistent than they had been, the alignment of

the unsupported back rail could still vary by a large amount. For this reason most Seven fitters stuck to the time-honoured method of using a knee to bend the hood sticks to suit each particular car.

In 1961 Ford supplemented their range of modern four-cylinder engines with the introduction of the 1,340cc 109E Classic. The styling of the car didn't go down too well but the engine was another matter. Fred Bushell, Managing Director of Lotus Cars, was one of the first people to take delivery of a Ford Classic and the engine bay soon came in for close scrutiny in the company car park. Here was yet another power unit ideal for fitting in the Seven.

The first person to fit the 1340 engine in a Seven was Warren King, owner of the first production Series 1. In 1961 he was working in the accounts department at Cheshunt and, being very keen to update his Seven, sought Mike Costin's advice. Costin

Warren King's car, formerly FVV 877, in S1½ form, with flared wings but retaining the S1 droop snoot. King revised the facia, placing the speedo and tacho together, some six years before Lotus did this on the S3. He was also the first person to fit a Seven with a Ford Classic 1,340cc engine.

A 1961 S2, showing the interior with the speedometer mounted on the passenger side of the snug cockpit. At this point the Seven still had a side-exit exhaust, a feature that remained until 1963.

Designed by Lotus employee Warren King for his own car, sidescreens were copied by Lotus Components and offered as a £7 10s option on the S2 Seven in 1961. The hood fit was improved at the same time to bring a level of weather protection unknown to most early Seven drivers.

Right up to the S3 Seven, the fuel filler remained in the Seven's boot, where the level could be checked either with a rod or simply by peering inside.

enthused over the virtues of the 109E engine and King duly acquired one, complete with the associated four-speed gearbox. He modified the mountings to accommodate the engine, which he equipped with a single SU carburettor and a Cosworth cam that Keith Duckworth had been able to provide. At the same time, King fitted his Seven with flared wings, sidescreens and a heater as well as redesigning the dashboard so that the speedometer and tachometer were side by side directly in front of the driver.

King's car sat daily in the company car park, and the new sidescreens attracted the attention of Lotus Components. The screens were a simple but effective design that King and his friend Tony Caldersmith, head of Lotus Service, had sketched out and had made up. They comprised a vinyl-covered steel frame which pivoted on two small hinges bolted to the windscreen pillars. Seven motoring suddenly became quite civilized. Lotus Components borrowed the design for the production Sevens, redesigning them to hang on simple nylon hinges with a brass pivot pin. King never received so much as a word of thanks for the idea!

The Ford 1500 pre-crossflow engine as offered in the S2 Seven. This view of a display unit shows the Triumph remote gearchange grafted onto the Ford gearbox with an adaptor plate.

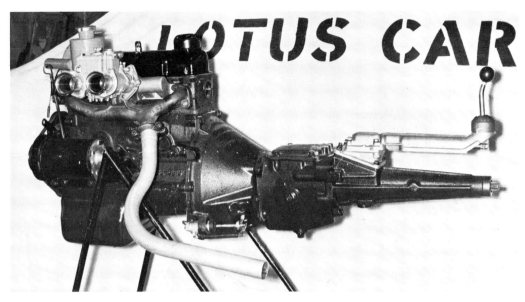

Colin Chapman seldom drove Sevens after the early days but here he is demonstrating an S2 Seven to an alarmed looking journalist at the Guild of Motoring Writers test day in 1961.

With the introduction of the 109E-powered Seven, Lotus reactivated the lapsed Super Seven name tag and offered a Cosworth modified 1,340cc unit as standard, clearly identified by the attractive sand-cast rocker cover bearing Cosworth's name. With a worked head, Cosworth cam, twin Weber carburettors and a four-branch manifold, this tremendously free-revving engine produced an untemperamental 85bhp. However, the version fitted to 8843 AR, the S2 Seven that subsequently went out for road test in the hands of various motoring magazines, was reputed to be somewhat more powerful. Lotus were not averse to making sure of good test results in this way.

At this point a 'swirl pot' was added to the cooling system for the first time to increase the system's capacity and make it more effective. There wasn't room at the front of the chassis to fit any sort of engine-driven cooling fan, so the introduction of an optional electric fan on UK cars was timely. Sevens had previously had a reputation as 'boilers' and many owners had fitted their own DIY electric fan system.

The new Super Seven of 1961 cost £599 in kit form and understandably received rave reviews. Top speed was around 100mph and acceleration to 60mph took just eight seconds, or even less, depending on whose road test results you believe. This made it one of the fastest cars around. In the words of *The Motor* it offered: 'Phenomenal Performance for the Hardy Handyman.'

The specification of the S2 was gradually improved right through its life. Items like the hood, sidescreens, tachometer and cooling fan, all once options, became standard equipment while the list of other options, be they extra instruments or more engine add-ons, became longer.

Detail engineering changes occurred slowly at Cheshunt. As Don Gadd, who ran the development workshop, recalls: 'The development department was preoccupied with racing cars. Jobs to do with the touring cars would quite often get left until last. Come Saturday morning just before knocking off time, someone would say hadn't we better do something about the new gearbox for the Seven..?'

The 1962 London Motor Show saw the introduction of the final engine to be offered as standard in the S2. It was yet another Ford unit, this time from the Cortina, and gave the Seven its largest displacement engine yet at 1,498cc.

In standard form the latest 'Super Seven' had this engine in 66bhp tune, but there was a Cosworth version too, with a mighty 95bhp. The standard specification had an unmodified engine with a single Weber carburettor but the Cosworth version had much higher compression, fully worked head, Cosworth camshaft, four-branch manifold and twin Weber carburettors. No wonder this was the most rapid Seven yet, with a 0-60 time of a shade under seven seconds and a top speed of almost 103mph. This power was coupled with plenty of torque. The car was so light that one of the standard demonstrations used by the Lotus salesmen was to come to halt and then pull away again smoothly in fourth gear.

Sales Manager Peter Warr had another occasion to demonstrate the lightness of a Seven. 'I was taking a potential customer for a ride in the demonstrator and we were hammering down a country lane outside Cheshunt when it started to rain. The wiper switch on the S2 is right next to the steering wheel and I just stretched out a finger and clicked it on. The wipers didn't work. We never let on to a customer that something on a car didn't work, so I surreptitiously switched off again. The screen got wetter and wetter and I kept saying things like, "Oh, it's not bad enough yet for the wipers." Finally I just couldn't see anything and we came to a corner and just slid off the road! We went up a bank and landed with all four wheels off the ground, resting on the undertray. I had to ask the potential customer to help me lift the car back down to the road again! He actually bought one.'

The advent of the Super Seven 1500 saw the introduction of an improved hood in vinyl with rear three-quarter windows, while for the first time a heater was available as an option at £17 10s. In standard form the model sold for £585. Opting for the Cosworth specification bumped the price up to £645. As far as gearboxes were concerned, the basic Cortina unit was the one normally fitted, but the closer ratios of the Cortina GT box were available for £40 extra and were recommended for use with the Cosworth-tuned engine.

The rear axle remained the long-suffering Standard unit and it should be said that with these higher power outputs, differential failures were becoming more common. The twisting forces fed into the axle either broke the casing or distorted it to the extent that the oil escaped and it seized.

With the introduction of the Super Seven 1500 the exhaust was routed right to the back of the car for the first time. Similarly the

Tail first as a unit is the time-honoured method of installing the engine and gearbox in a Seven chassis. This is a Ford 1500 unit being fitted to a car destined for export fully assembled.

1500 was at last fitted with lights that dipped in the modern fashion and made night driving a rather less terrifying experience. However, there were still no indicators; they would have to wait a few years yet, and a fuel gauge still wasn't available. The 1500 was fitted with front disc brakes from the Triumph

Spitfire: the Seven's stopping power increased dramatically as a result.

Each change in engine specification seemed to give the Seven a new lease of life. Former Managing Director Fred Bushell was later to reflect, 'The company stopped putting its shoulder to the wheel with the Seven not very long after the move to Cheshunt. The car had a steady but limited market and Components needed a steady product, so they just kept on building it. It needed very little input from Colin and after we'd sorted out the basic specification it just kept ticking over.'

'Ticking over' in those first few years at Cheshunt meant producing an average of seven cars per week. The build records for a couple of months in 1962 read 2,10, 6, 7, 8, 3, 9, 6, with the low totals occuring in weeks when complete cars were being built for export. That the Seven was only ticking over is illustrated by the fact that between 1964 and 1968 no major motoring magazine conducted a road test of one.

Buyers of Seven kits were offered a post-build inspection and indeed several insurance companies made this a condition of insuring the car. There was a check list of points against which a car presented for inspection was marked. The inspector wasn't allowed to do anything about any faults he discovered apart from point them out. To do otherwise constituted 'professional assistance'. Assembly of the Seven still had to be an amateur operation otherwise dreaded purchase tax raised its ugly head.

However, there were exceptions. Roy Badcock, who by 1964 was Workshop Manager of Lotus Components, remembers one particular customer arriving at Cheshunt and presenting his just-completed car for inspection. 'We discovered that the steering column was held into the rack coupling by only 2mm of spline. On the basis that this bloke would probably be killed if he drove the car home in that condition, we took out the coupling bolt, and put the shaft in properly.' Fortunately the Inland Revenue inspector didn't visit Cheshunt that day.

Former Sales Manager Peter Warr was made General Manager of Lotus Components in 1962, following the untimely death from a heart attack of Nobby Clarke, Lotus's first full-time employee. Warr found that the organization of Seven production still left something to be desired. 'There were plenty of clangers dropped during production. There were an awful lot of car parts flying round the factory as we tried to sort things out. Friday was

At speed in an S2 demonstrator, quite possibly the legendary KAR 120C. Just before this shot was taken the ignition switch had jammed and the car had been 'hot wired'—hence the lack of keys in the switch!

particularly bad because that was the normal delivery day and sometimes we'd shift as many as five kits. Just when it all seemed over, we'd suddenly find a pile of bits out in the yard that someone had left behind. After we'd sorted that out, we'd find that one chap had gone off with someone else's chassis or had taken a car with completely the wrong specification! Great fun though!'

One of the real problems that Warr encountered was that of sourcing parts for the Seven. 'There was a stage when parts were so short that there was thought of reverting to the Lotus 6 era – you buy the chassis body unit and the special Lotus parts, then we give you a list and off you go and buy all the other bits retail.' However, this idea was quickly forgotten when the parts supply situation recovered.

At Cheshunt, while the Seven was being built steadily upstairs in Components' factory, the fitters downstairs were busy building single seaters and sports racing cars including the highly successful 23 and 23B. Lotus Cars meanwhile phased out the Elite and concentrated on the Elan which in S2 form in 1964 at last started to make some money for the factory. Lotus narrowly missed out on being awarded the contract to build and develop the GT40 for Ford, but were given the highly profitable and

A lasting memory and still an inspiration for many Seven owners was the appearance of KAR 120C in the TV series 'The Prisoner'. Two KARs appeared, the 'real' one, normally the Lotus demonstrator, and a second lookalike seen here with the Prisoner himself, Patrick McGoohan, and Graham Nearn of Caterham Cars. McGoohan repaid Caterham's efforts in preparing a car for filming virtually overnight by posing for a series of photographs that were used in advertisements for some time after.

prestigious job of building almost 3,000 Lotus Cortinas. Lotus was suddenly very big business.

Team Lotus too were enjoying a golden era in Grand Prix racing; Jim Clark was World Champion in 1963 and nearly managed it again in 1964. Then in 1965 Clark won the Championship again and added Indianapolis to his string of successes for good measure. The atmosphere among the workforce at Cheshunt at times verged on the euphoric. Turnover was up, profit was up; it seemed as though Lotus could do no wrong.

And still the Lotus Seven soldiered on. In 1965, sales received a useful lift when the Lotus S2 demonstrator, registered KAR 120C, appeared in the hugely successful and mysterious TV series called *The Prisoner*, starring former Dangerman, Patrick McGoohan. It was McGoohan himself who contacted Lotus

Marketing Director, Graham Arnold, to ask for the loan of an Elan for use in the series. Never one to overlook a good promotional opportunity, the ebullient Arnold arranged for McGoohan to have sight of both an Elan and a Seven. The upshot of this was that McGoohan chose the Seven, which suited Arnold admirably as an Elan was already being used by Emma Peel in *The Avengers*. As prisoner Number 6 in 'The Village' where the series was based, McGoohan should really have driven a Mark 6, but having the Seven just added to the mystery of it all.

KAR 120C appeared at the beginning and end of each of the 20 episodes and during the action in at least three episodes. During the opening sequence the car was static against a moving backdrop. The following footage was shot in one of the tunnels at Heathrow airport and purportedly showed McGoohan in the

Seven roaring down to his Controller's headquarters to tender his resignation, thus precipitating his abduction to 'The Village'.

KAR 120C had already been delivered back to Lotus and sold when McGoohan came on to Arnold to ask for the car back again at short notice for a final scene to be shot. There was no car available at Cheshunt but Caterham Cars were able to help out. The real KAR 120C had been Cosworth 1500-powered, but Caterham's David Wakefield and his workshop team worked through the night to convert an older 105E-engined Seven to look like KAR 120C. The substitute car was painted green with yellow nosecone and had such details as stoneguards on the lights. It was this car that appeared in the final episode of the series when McGoohan returns to London from 'The Village'.

Graham Nearn of Caterham Cars drove the car to the set for the final episode to be shot and found himself recruited as an actor for the day. He can be seen dusting off the car and posting the keys through McGoohan's letter box, prior to the hero's arrival. After all the filming was done, McGoohan found time to be photographed with Nearn and the Seven. The pictures that resulted appeared in Caterham Cars' advertisements for a long time after.

KAR 120C had been the Lotus demonstrator up to its appearance in *The Prisoner*. By 1965, not much effort was being put into selling Sevens and the salesmen were much more interested in pushing the Elan instead. Consequently, KAR used to sit 'out the back' on partially flat tyres from week to week. A former employee recalled: 'KAR would sit there until someone came in and absolutely insisted on having a test ride in a Seven. The salesman would show him the car, let him sit in it and then go away and have a cup of coffee or something. He'd then peer out through the sales office blinds and if the customer was still sitting in the car, maybe relent and go and see if the engine would fire up. Yes, it's true to say that we didn't try very hard to sell the Seven during the last year at Cheshunt!'

Meanwhile, Colin Chapman was so delighted at Jim Clark's Indianapolis victory that all Clark's mechanics were given Cortinas as a reward. Dick Scammel didn't want his and sold it to Warren King, prompting King to sell his historic Seven, chassis 401. David Lazenby, Clark's Chief Mechanic, was to be the most highly rewarded and was offered the job of General Manager of Lotus Components. Peter Warr by this time had decided to leave

as he didn't want to move with Lotus to the new factory in Norfolk. It had been common knowledge for some time that another factory move was in the air. Lazenby wasn't totally enthusiastic about the new job as he had hitherto avoided 'admin,' but nevertheless, towards the end of '65 he took up the new position.

Between 1964 and 1968, though Lotus Cars continued on the up and up, Lotus Components were not to enjoy such a fruitful period. While Colin Chapman had been empire building, his contemporaries carried on in their own way building racing cars and little else, becoming very good at it. The original aim of Lotus – building racing cars – got rather left behind as the other parts of the company steamed ahead.

Lotus continued to build successful cars for its own team but when it came to customer cars things were not so good in the face of smaller specialist opposition. While Lotus Components should have been cashing in much more on Jim Clark's success, sales were being lost to firms such as Brabham. The Lotus 11, 18, 20, 22 and 23 were all relatively big sellers. But with the advent of the specialized and expensive technique of monocoque construction, fewer privateers were running racing teams. Lotus models such as the 27, 32, and 35 sold only in small numbers. The spaceframe 31 and 41 recovered the situation somewhat, but the underlying trend was still not in the right direction. The Seven, as ever, continued to sell steadily, but the costs of production had risen and it was no longer making money although it still performed a useful function in turning over revenue.

Basically, Lotus Components needed a new car and Colin Chapman had come up with a scheme as early as 1964. The type 46, later known as the Europa, was designed to be Lotus Components' new car. Never one to miss the opportunity of learning from others, Chapman drew inspiration for the 46 from a Ford styling exercise. The new car was to be a Seven in the modern idiom; fast, attractive and, most importantly, very simple and cheap to build.

The chassis was a backbone design, similar to the Elan, with a sleek glassfibre body bonded to it. The engine however was a simple Renault unit mounted amidships with the cleverly adapted Renault gearbox behind. Interior trim was minimal and the windows didn't even open. But things didn't go according to plan: the prototype was built by Lotus Developments in 1964 but

Sevens for America. A batch of Sevens heading for USA distributor Jay Chamberlain in 1961, each with the chassis number marked on its identification board. All the cars shipped to Chamberlain were right-hand drive although the first S2 had been a left-hand drive prototype. LHD cars didn't come on stream until 1963. Californian-registered car above has Elan-style perforated steel wheels.

got the thumbs down for looks and practicality. The 46 went back for a rethink, to emerge three years later as a very different car; one that Lotus Cars wanted for themselves. Lotus Components would have to look elsewhere for their future. Lazenby in the meantime pursued the idea of resurrecting the Elite and fitting it with a Twin Cam engine but the idea never got beyond the construction of one prototype.

By 1965, after just six years at Cheshunt, Lotus had outgrown its site and there was no room left to expand. Another factory move was imminent. What Chapman had in mind this time was not quite as simple as the move from Hornsey to Cheshunt. He

had located a site adjacent to a disused airfield at a place called Hethel in the wilds of Norfolk. Chapman was sufficiently aware of his own charisma to know that the majority of the Cheshunt staff would follow him. Many of the men from the very early Hornsey days were still with him.

However, there were a few key members of staff who were less enamoured of the proposed move. Peter Warr, for one, decided to leave. Group Purchasing Manager Mike Warner was also not too happy. In the end Chapman sold the move to Warner by flying him over Hethel in the company aircraft and describing most vividly how wonderful the new air-conditioned factory was going to be. Warner recalls Chapman saying with a flourish at 2,000 feet: 'Well there it is, isn't it marvellous...' The overgrown airfield, speckled with rusting farm machinery and the yokel swinging on a gate, waving up at the plane, didn't impress Warner unduly, but he signed up nonetheless, whereupon he was given the task of co-ordinating the factory move.

In October 1966, the entire Lotus Operation moved to the new factory which mainly comprised a great open-plan, hangar-like structure. Lotus Components duly established their workshop at the opposite end of the factory to Lotus Cars' production line. Just before the move to Hethel, Sales Director Graham Arnold

had told Graham Nearn of Caterham Cars that the Seven was about to be axed. The Europa was on the way, along with the Elan Plus 2, both of which were indicative of what Chapman was later to refer to as 'a lurch up market'. There was a growing feeling that the Seven no longer really fitted into the scheme of things; maybe reminding customers too much of the company's humble origins. Besides which, sales of the Seven were at a very low level.

Graham Nearn was quick to respond once he saw the building of Sevens really had stopped; he ordered 20 cars and Lotus started building the Seven again, having let it lapse for several months following the move to Norfolk, almost hoping that they

Mike Warner left Lotus in 1968 to found his own company making wheels; part of the deal that persuaded him to return to Lotus as head of Components was that Lotus bought out the wheel company, resulting in the attractive range of Brand Lotus wheels.

57

could let it die without anyone noticing. Former Managing Director, Fred Bushell, recalls how every time the board sat down for a meeting at which officially axing the Seven was on the agenda, someone would walk through the door with an order. 'We just couldn't bring ourselves to turn down ready money.'

Some time before the move to Hethel, the contract to produce the Seven chassis was transferred from Universal Radiators to Arch Motors. For years, Don Gadd, who ran the development shop at Cheshunt, had been trying to convince Colin Chapman of the benefits of using bronze welding rather than fusion welding to build up spaceframes. But it took ages for Chapman to allow even secondary tubes to be joined in this way. When it became clear that bronze welding was every bit as strong as fusion welding and caused less distortion of the tubes, thus giving greater accuracy, Chapman at last relented. Arch Motors, great proponents of this welding technique, were given the contract. Another company started aluminium panelling Seven chassis at around this time.

Eve and Son of Norwich began by cladding the occasional chassis for Lotus, but soon were to take over the whole contract.

In 1967, Caterham Cars boss Graham Nearn went to Lotus with a proposal to take on the sole distributorship of the Seven. Sales Director Graham Arnold liked the idea and the deal was struck. Meanwhile Lotus Components as a whole continued to mark time. Something had to happen. Colin Chapman was convinced that Components could make money and in May 1968 came up with a plan. This involved former Group Purchasing Director Mike Warner. Warner had left Lotus in late 1967 at the expiry of his contract and had set up his own company making a range of light alloy wheels. The invitation he accepted to lunch with Fred Bushell and Colin Chapman led to an offer to return to Lotus as Chief Executive of Lotus Components. The proposed deal was so good that he couldn't refuse. In April '68 he was back at Hethel to set about revitalizing Lotus Components – and that included doing something with the Seven.

The demonstrator fleet at the Cheshunt factory in 1965, including the 'Prisoner' car. Note the popularity of '120' registration numbers: Sales Director Graham Arnold maintained that this hinted at the cars' top speeds.

CHAPTER 5

Further development

The Seven Series 3 1968-1969

With the advent of Formula Ford racing, it looked as if salvation was at hand for Lotus Components. The company was presented with a highly profitable new avenue to explore. The motor racing school at Brands Hatch had come up with an idea for a junior racing formula called Formula Ford. School boss Geoff Clarke and Brands Hatch boss John Webb set about finding a manufacturer to build a run of cars suitable for the new formula. They met with Colin Chapman in March 1967 and it was agreed that Lotus would build 25 Formula Fords. Thus the Lotus 51 came about.

The first-ever Formula Ford race was an entirely Lotus affair and took place in July 1967. Coincidentally, leader on the first lap and also the first man to spin off in Formula Ford was George Lewis, son of Edward Lewis, recipient of the very first Seven.

Although Lotus had Formula Ford to themselves at first, other manufacturers were soon snapping at their heels. Nevertheless, building the new spaceframe racer at least gave Components a sound base upon which to look to the future: but their financial performance was still poor.

When Mike Warner arrived to take over as Chief Executive of Components in 1968, he had very definite and ambitious plans for the way business should develop. David Lazenby, as General Manager of Components, was left in a somewhat invidious position with Warner brought in above him and, although the two men got on well, was to resign six months later.

Every inch the dynamic young executive, 28-year old Warner's plan was to tackle the construction and marketing of racing cars in a more professional manner than anyone had hitherto attempted. His brief was to turn the company round and in the normal Chapman fashion he was allowed plenty of scope to do this as he saw fit. Formula Ford production was organized on a production line basis. Plans were laid for new improved models including the Lotus 59 Formula 3 car. With so much activity, and a breath of fresh air hitting the company, the 70-strong Components workforce was revitalized.

The Seven, still being produced in S2 guise, was not exempt from these changes. Right from the start Warner had petitioned his fellow directors on the Lotus board to sign off permission to develop a revised Seven. The answer had been a most definite thumbs down. While not abandoning the scheme for a very different Seven, Components did the next best thing and set about revamping the car to inject some life back into sales which had settled back to a modest level.

To a large extent the man responsible for the Seven S3 was Graham Nearn. As sole concessionaire for the Seven he had taken to visiting Hethel every week to collect his quota of cars on a Land-Rover and trailer and generally keep an eye on what was going on. In early 1968 he presented a proposal to the Lotus board containing ideas about how the Seven should develop and how it should be marketed. Colin Chapman in particular was impressed with this document and confirmed that Caterham Cars would remain sole distributors of the Seven. This came as a relief to Nearn, because on one of his weekly visits to Hethel, he had got wind of a plan to reorganize the distribution of the Seven and feared for his position. However, his suggestions for fitting the latest Ford engine, uprating the equipment specification and maybe producing a limited edition Seven were well received and his sole distributorship was assured.

In the early summer of 1968, Lotus staged one of the now

After a batch of interim Sevens known as the S2½, using the Ford 1600 crossflow engine with the last of the Standard axles, the true S3 Seven with the Ford axle arrived in August 1968. The chassis was basic S2 but there were many detail changes—wider wheels, new exhaust, exterior fuel filler and revised instrumentation not least among them.

familiar Open Days at Hethel. One of the attractions on the day was a so-called world record attempt at assembling a Seven from a kit. The man who tackled this public feat was Seven fitter, John Robinson, and he took just over four hours. It was discovered some time later that Robinson had taken the precaution of assembling the car beforehand to make sure that everything fitted and then taken it to bits again. Graham Nearn was overseeing the 'record' and the only way he could stop Robinson bolting the car together in a preposterously short time was to keep sending him on tea breaks. The four hours or so that became the official record was at least believable.

A time-honoured way of enlivening interest in a long-established model is to uprate it in some way and give it a new designation. Motoring magazines will then road test it again and the marketing men have something new to trumpet about and upon which to base advertising and PR campaigns. And this is what happened with the Seven in 1968.

Ford, long-time provider of engines suitable for the Seven, had replaced the Cortina's 1,500cc unit with two new versions of 1,300 and 1,600cc, designated 225E. Both these new units were

particularly appealing designs with efficient crossflow cylinder heads in which the exhaust and inlet manifolds were mounted on opposite sides, whereas on the pre-crossflow units, both had been on the left side of the head. In standard single-carburettor form the 1600 Cortina engine produced 84bhp; not too much less than tuned 1500s, so uprated versions of the larger engines looked very promising indeed. Both were specified for the new version of the Seven. In the changeover period between the S2 and the S3, a handful of interim S2s were fitted with this larger Ford engine. The last S2s proper had 1,500cc Cosworth engines, but without the Cosworth rocker cover as Cosworth suddenly decided to make them 'unavailable.'

It is interesting to note that John Robinson, who was responsible for assembling the first 1600 crossflow Seven in 1968, entered it on the build sheet as the 'New Seven', calling it the '2½' for good measure. Nowadays, '2½s' are taken to be 1,600cc cars with the last of the Standard axles.

Apart from the change of basic power unit, there was an important change of rear axle with the advent of the S3. The Standard Companion had been defunct for many years, but until

The intake on the bonnet of the S3 was to
cover the 'pancake' air filter of the single
carburettor Ford crossflow engine.

1968 Lotus had been able to obtain Companion axles for use in the Seven. Caterham Cars occasionally located and delivered them to Lotus simply to keep production going. However, supplies started to dry up at long last and a new axle was needed. The possibility of taking over the tooling for the Standard axle was investigated but ruled out on grounds of cost. Besides which, the old axle was already being stressed way beyond its design capabilities, so that with even more powerful engines on the way, failures would become even more common. To some extent the problem had been relieved by the introduction of a reinforcing plate welded to the back of the casing. Ron Davies at Caterham Cars had pioneered this technique and Lotus subsequently adopted it, but it didn't face up to the basic fact that a stronger axle was needed.

Lotus already had strong associations with Ford, so where better to look for a new axle than the Ford Escort? The one selected as being the best for the job was that from the Escort Mexico. However, fitting it wasn't entirely straightforward because it was both wider than the Standard axle and the wheel stud spacings were different. The width problem was easily overcome by making the rear wings wider to cover the wheels. Matching the front hubs with the rears meant commissioning a new hub assembly to combine with the Triumph uprights. The Ford axle had stronger halfshafts than the Standard unit but a question mark still hung over the strength of the casing so the reinforcing plate remained. The propshaft was redesigned to link up with the new axle. Changing to Ford hubs allowed Lotus Cortina wheels to be specified for the Seven which was a step in the right direction as their width was 5½in compared to the 5in rims of the later S2s. The Ford axle came with a 3.77:1 final drive as standard, but a 4.12:1 was optionally available.

Disc front brakes, first seen on the S2 Super Seven, became standard for the S3. The rear drum brakes associated with the Escort axle were wider than the Standard drums and offered a useful increase in braking power. The crossflow design of the S3's engine meant that the inlet manifold was on the right-hand side of the car for the first time. The downdraught Weber stood proud of the engine, so a small intake cowl in glassfibre, painted silver, was added to the bonnet to cover the 'pancake' air filter.

In an attempt both to make the S3 quieter and to reduce the

A side shot of the first S3 just before its launch. The use of wider wheels and tyres gave this Seven a more aggressive look than the S2.

Another early S3 photographed on the test track at the Hethel factory. This car has Brand Lotus wheels and left-hand drive.

likelihood of passengers catching an ankle on the side-mounted exhaust, the standard S3 system had a shorter but fatter silencer box mounted further forward, under the front wing. The pipe from the rear of the silencer box kinked downwards to be as inconspicuous as possible.

The instrumentation came in for major reorganization with the S3. A tachometer, now standard, was mounted next to the speedometer directly in front of the driver, with the supplementary dials on either side. At last these included a fuel gauge since a sender unit had finally been designed to fit in the tank top. Refuelling was given some attention at this point too, and the filler neck was moved to protrude through the back panel, having a right-angled rubber hose connecting it to the tank. In reality this made life harder when refuelling. No longer was it necessary to unload the boot in order to replenish the tank, but the new arrangement brought the problem of splashback. S3 owners soon became used to having their shoes doused with petrol.

An electric fan became standard for the S3, operated by one of a collection of unidentified toggle switches. Indicators became standard, those at the front mounted beneath the headlights on a cleverly redesigned bracket. The concept of 'any colour trim as long as it's red' had been phased out mid-way through the life of the S2. The S3 had black PVC trim as standard with footwell carpets also in black; luxury indeed!

The list of optional extras included such items as a limited-slip differential, close-ratio gearbox, roll-over bar, oil cooler, heater and seat belts, mounting points for which had been built into the S3 chassis.

Apart from the seat belt mountings and changes in bracketry to suit the new axle, the S3 chassis was the same as the S2 and was still produced by Arch Motors. The S3 was maybe 200lb heavier than its older brother and the engine was more powerful too. For these reasons the chassis of the S3 Seven and indeed the later S2 versions might usefully have been improved and made stiffer.

Caterham cars had become sole distributor of the Seven in 1967. This was their first S3 demonstrator, in 1968. Unusually it remained in bare aluminium but had green glassfibre wings and nose.

Nevertheless, the Seven could still run rings round almost every other sports car, without really trying.

The first S3 was complete by August 1968. Pre-warned of its arrival, Graham Nearn had planned a small launch party, announcing the event in his regular page 1 advertisement in *Motor Sport* magazine. The venue selected was the Ringlestone Arms pub, owned by Nearn's brother, in the village of Ringlestone. A handful of hardy enthusiasts had been expected to turn up. However, continuous drizzle notwithstanding, the Ringlestone Arms was that evening besieged by a sea of people all desperate for a glimpse of the new car.

The Seven that they saw was certainly a beauty, finished in metallic blue and perfectly prepared. It had been delivered by transporter that evening. The protective polythene wrapping had

been stripped away and the car hidden in a nearby barn. It was then discovered that the rotor arm had been removed by Lotus so that it couldn't be driven. Nearn was having none of that and acquired a suitable rotor arm from another Seven in the car park. This was duly installed, and at the appointed hour the engine was fired up and the Seven driven out of the barn to be greeted by the appreciative masses. Three orders for S3s were taken on that night alone and there was a steady flood of inquiries for weeks after based on the success of that initial launch.

The cars that Caterham sold were offered in three forms. Overseas customers still had the option to buy a Seven complete and running. But purchase tax still applied to completed cars in the UK, so for the home market most Sevens were offered in one of two kit forms. Stage one was the basic kit comprising a partially fitted-out chassis and several boxes of bits. The stage two kit was rather more advanced and took pre-assembly as far as possible without attracting the attention of the men from the Inland Revenue.

Sales of the S3 were running at an average of five cars per week, but Mike Warner was still pushing his idea for a more fundamentally revised Seven. His arguments at Board meetings worked better this time round, because Colin Chapman acquiesced and gave him the go-ahead, albeit on a ridiculously small budget of £5,000. Warner was not to be put off by this. He set designers Peter Lucas, Dave Baldwin and Alan Barrett on the project full-time, leaving the S3 Seven to keep things ticking over.

Lotus Components had an exclusive tie-up with engine tuners Holbay to produce Formula Ford engines. A fruit of this association was that Holbay were able to supply tuning parts for the Cortina engine as fitted to the Seven. The full Holbay-spec engine was balanced and had a gas-flowed cylinder head, high-lift camshaft, special pistons and 10:1 compression ratio. There was a four-branch exhaust manifold and twin 40 DCOE Weber carburettors mounted on a specially cast inlet manifold. At 6,200rpm the Holbay modified engine was rated at 120bhp which made a car so fitted quite comfortably the most powerful Seven yet, although the greater weight of the S3 meant that its performance wasn't very much more than the Cosworth S2.

For the January 1969 Racing Car Show in London, Lotus Components produced an 'Ultimate Seven' show car. This was christened the Seven S. It was fitted with the full-spec Holbay engine, matched by an uprating of the trim and fittings to a level not previously associated with the model. The bodywork was finished in Rolls-Royce Regal Red and the visible suspension components were chromed. The once PVC covered facia was now finished in attractive burnished aluminium. Plush piped-

Boss of Lotus Components Mike Warner (left) retained a strong interest in Sevens. Here he is handing a model of a Seven to a participant in a Lotus Seven Club meeting at Hethel.

Lotus signed a deal in 1969 with a group of South American businessmen for the Seven to be assembled in Argentina. The Argentine Seven used a Fiat engine, hence the bonnet bulge on the other side of the bonnet from the normal Ford-powered cars. In the event, only a handful of cars emerged from this arrangement.

edge wool carpets came as standard, extending over the transmission tunnel for the first time. The seats were contoured and well padded with the inner side panels finished in a matching shade of ivory; quite a contrast to the normal black. Even the gearlever had a neat little ivory-coloured shroud and the hood too conformed to the colour scheme. Seatbelts were standard, as were air horns and a heater.

The Seven S even went so far as to have a radio mounted above the driver's right knee, with the speaker fitted in the boot. The Dunlop SP tyres were mounted on Brand Lotus alloys wheels. Manufactured by GKN, these wheels had been designed by the company Mike Warner had founded when he left Lotus back in 1967. As part of the deal to persuade Warner to rejoin Lotus, Colin Chapman agreed to take over the enterprise.

As shown at the 1969 Racing Car Show, the Seven S bore a price tag of no less than £1,600. The Show car was tested by *Car* magazine as a production model in August 1969, but in fact only the one true 'S' was built, although many Sevens were sold with the S-spec engine and some of the options. *Car* recorded a top speed of 108mph and acceleration to 60mph in 7.4 seconds. With

average fuel consumption at 18.4mpg, they thought the Seven S was thirsty as well as very expensive.

1969 was something of a vintage year for Seven sales, with more than 200 new cars passing through Caterham Cars' hands. The cash that this generated for Lotus Components went a long way to funding the development of the S4 which was coming on apace. Another potentially profitable avenue that Mike Warner investigated around this time was the establishment of licensing agreements to produce the Seven in other countries. An approach by three South Americans by the names of Boschi, Mutio and Vignoles led to Warner, and subsequently Colin Chapman, visiting Argentina to sign an agreement for Lotus Seven kits to be assembled in Buenos Aires and fitted with Fiat engines. Interestingly, these Sevens were to retain the Lotus badge. As with almost every other arrangement of this type, the project fizzled out and only a handful of Argentinian Sevens were made. The licence lapsed after three years.

Meanwhile, back in the UK, there was one final version of the S3 still to come. The official factory position over the fitting of the Lotus Twin Cam engine into the Seven was that it wouldn't fit.

The 'Ultimate' S3 Seven was the SS which at last saw a Seven fitted with a Lotus Twin Cam engine. The chassis was strengthened to cope with the extra power and the first example was panelled in steel rather than aluminium. With special wheels, high-spec interior and red trim, the white car was a real eye-catcher at the 1969 Motor Show. The bonnet was cut away to display the engine but, to the annoyance of all those who had built the car, this meant that it wasn't judged for the coachwork competition.

The well-stocked engine compartment of the SS, with the 125bhp Holbay-assembled Lotus Twin Cam occupying the space originally designed for a wheezing Ford sidevalve unit!

Graham Nearn and many other Seven owners knew otherwise.

With the 1969 Motor Show just round the corner, Graham Nearn made one of his weekly visits to Hethel. But this time he turned up in a Seven into which an owner had fitted a Twin Cam engine from an Elan. Presented with clear proof that the Twin Cam would fit into a Seven, Lotus Components set about creating the Seven SS. The idea of using this engine was particularly appealing, because it was made in-house at Hethel and cost Lotus less than the 1600 Ford engine.

Fortunately for potential customers, the creation of the Twin Cam Seven involved rather more than simply welding up new engine mounts, dropping the engine in and tacking on SS badges. Owners of standard Sevens fitted with powerful engines and modern tyres were experiencing broken chassis tubes and finding that under certain conditions the car was 'lozenging'. One makeshift remedy was to weld collars onto the anti-roll bar to stop it moving from side to side as the chassis flexed but the result of this was often a broken bar.

Paying heed to these problems, Peter Lucas, head draughtsman of Lotus Components, amended an S2 chassis drawing in

A snapshot taken at 4 o'clock on the morning of the 1969 Motor Show's opening after the frantic rush to complete the Twin Cam SS show car. On the left of the group, in order from the left, are Alan Barrett, Peter Lucas, Peter Brand, Ken Robinson and Mike Warner.

glamour of the pre-war Jaguar SS. It should be said, however, that Jaguar dropped the designation because of its unfortunate wartime associations. Warner didn't think this was significant.

Visitors to the 1969 Motor Show liked what they saw; Graham Nearn took 13 Twin Cam SS orders along with deposits against the kit price of £1,225. Lotus Components set about making the cars to fulfil these orders. The production versions reverted from steel to aluminium panelling but retained the chassis strengthening.

Mike Warner took the show car, chassis 2564/TC1, for his personal use, although two years later he was to sell it to Graham Nearn who still owns it today and displays it in Caterham Cars' showroom. As the final S3 Sevens left Hethel in November 1969, so production of the 'traditional' Seven ended and Mike Warner's pet project took over. Thirteen is the official total of Twin Cam SS production, but as a former Components employee reflected, 'There was always the personal friend of Mr Chapman who wanted one and we couldn't turn him away...'

Autocar, which had been the first magazine ever to test a Seven, back in 1957, were also first to lay hands on a Twin Cam SS in late 1969. Surprisingly, VVF 7H managed only 103mph, with 60mph in 7.1 seconds; not very much different from the Holbay-tuned Ford-engined cars – the fact was that the Twin Cam cars weighed more than the Holbay-powered versions and had only 5bhp more – but the mid-range response was fierce and the handling and roadholding exceptionally good.

Mike Warner had certainly risen to the challenge of increasing production and efficiency at Lotus Components. Formula Fords, now in type 61 guise, were being made at an extraordinary rate. Sales Manager Graham Arnold, who had once quipped that Components could never produce sufficient cars for him to sell, now found himself in the position of having a log jam of racing cars. However, this was not of immediate significance to Mike Warner. Under the accounting system used by Lotus at that time, all the cars that Components made were sold internally to Lotus Sales and thus appeared as a credit on Components' books even if they weren't sold to the public.

Production of the S3 had ended in 1969, but new cars were still sold right through to the middle of 1970. Meanwhile, all eyes turned to the new Seven, the Series 4; a Seven for the 1970s.

red ball-point pen. He added triangulation in the engine bay and chassis side and made the stressed outer panels from welded steel rather than aluminium; hinting at the construction of the 'secret' S4 Seven. These three measures increased chassis strength quite significantly but put the weight up too. Arch Motors produced a chassis to this plan and a 125bhp Holbay-assembled Twin Cam was inserted. There was no time to get the car running before taking it to the Motor Show where it looked a real gem, finished in white with smartly trimmed interior and sitting on Brand Lotus wheels. The traditional side-mounted silencer with chromed shroud returned for the SS, which was distinctive in having the front indicators mounted on the sides of the nosecone rather than under the headlamp brackets. At the rear, Britax lights were recessed neatly into the wings.

The name 'SS' was selected by Warner not only because it harked back to the Super Seven but also because it hinted at the

CHAPTER 6

A Seven for the 1970s

The Seven Series 4 1970-1973

Back in 1964, the Lotus Europa had been earmarked as the 'new' Seven to be produced by Lotus Components. But the concept of it as an ultra-cheap mid-engined sports car changed and the Europa was produced instead by the main Lotus Cars factory at Hethel. Mike Warner, boss of Lotus Components, found, as had previous heads of the company, that he needed to produce a road car alongside the racing cars to compensate for the ups and downs of the racing car market. It was vital to bring money in from a constant source and the only such source available was the trusty Lotus Seven which just seemed to keep on selling.

Lotus Components were competing in the racing car market against small companies with tremendous flexibility, who could survive the off-season when there was no demand for racing cars. Lotus Components on the other hand were operating within a totally different financial environment. At Hethel, group over-heads had to be met regardless of the state of the racing car market. 'We were paying £30,000 a year towards company aircraft alone,' remembers Warner. 'The pressure was on.'

But Warner was full of confidence. In his first year running Lotus Components, he'd turned a £38,000 loss into a £10,000 profit and turnover was up by 50%. His plan of attack for the future was on several fronts. First, he cut the amount of floorspace occupied by Lotus Components, which meant that the company's contribution to central overheads was proportionally reduced. He then planned that Lotus Components would move to a refurbished factory on the periphery of the Hethel site where overheads would be lower still.

A new Lotus Seven was a cornerstone in his recovery plan. Warner's idea was not just for Components to produce the car, but also for them to market it in much larger quantities than ever before, through a new dealer network. At the same time, Lotus Components would change its name to Lotus Racing, which in truth gave a much better idea of what the company actually did.

Mike Warner had joined Lotus in 1960, having served an apprenticeship as a mechanical engineer. Initially he worked on the electrics of the Elite. Then he moved on to work in the inspection department, where one of his occasional tasks was examining kit cars that had come back for a post-build checkover. An early encounter with a Seven saw him overshooting a corner on the perimeter road of Pangshangar airfield and having an 'off' across a field wherein lay a length of angle-iron imbedded in the ground. The Seven caught the angle-iron on the undertray which opened like a tin can. Warner survived intact but reflects now that it was maybe that incident that implanted in him the desire to create a Seven that didn't have a flimsy aluminium floor!

From test inspector he moved on to work on development of the Lotus Cortina and Elan, before eventually rising to become Group Purchasing Manager, in which position he excelled. Hence the 1968 offer to persuade him to return to the company as Chief Executive of Lotus Components.

Warner's approach to problems was one of careful analysis. Soon after taking over Components he 'value engineered' the S3 Seven, an exercise that had never really been attempted before. This involved working out the true cost of every element that went into the car, including the labour component. The aim was to discover exactly where the money was being soaked up and see where savings could be made by re-engineering the car. What this exercise revealed in the case of the S3 Seven was that Lotus

OTUS RACING LIMITED

Components were losing between £100 and £110 on every one built. However, even at that level of loss it was still worthwhile producing the car, simply to achieve overhead recovery.

The bottom line of all this investigation into the S3 was that the parts needed to build it cost too much. Mike Warner recollects that the total cost of these was £380, against a selling price of around £1,200. For the Elan the respective figures he recalls as £445 and £2,300. In other words, the Seven sold for three times its basic price while the Elan sold for five times its parts cost. The figures did not make encouraging reading.

The most significant high cost factor on the Seven was the chassis. Back in 1957, when labour rates were relatively cheaper,

the fact that building the chassis was a very labour-intensive operation had been much less important than it was 12 years later. Each basic chassis frame was costing Lotus £55 at a time when the Elan chassis was being bought in for just £27. There was no way the Seven's chassis could be made more cheaply in its traditional form. Arch Motors were already supplying it at a rock bottom price, such was the pressure placed upon them by Lotus. 'Lotus seemed to think that we should be glad simply for the honour of doing work for them,' recalls boss of Arch, Bob Robinson. 'And then when we'd agreed to a price with virtually nil profit, they'd only pay the bill when they wanted another batch of chassis!'

An obvious route to explore for the Seven was that of redesigning it around the Elan's chassis. But, as a Director of Lotus, Warner was privileged to know that the Elan was only a short time away from being axed, so there was no future down that particular road. What the new car wanted was a chassis that could be produced simply and cheaply; one that didn't involve hand-beaten aluminium panelling. A proposal to create a new Seven around a widened Formula Ford chassis was considered briefly but this suggestion was quickly dropped.

By 1969, the time it took to prepare a Seven kit had been reduced dramatically from the 60 hours of the S1 right down to as little as 12 hours for the late S2 and S3s, but there seemed to be no way it could be reduced further. Fitting up the windscreen, wings, hood sticks and dash panel simply couldn't be tackled any faster. Trying to speed things up by putting two fitters on each car rather than one actually made the job slower as the two got in each other's way. These time-soaking aspects needed re-engineering if the Seven was ever to make any money.

There was also the legislation factor. Warner had maybe 2,000 cars per year in mind for production of the new Seven and recognized that many of these would have to be exported. The S3 seemed unlikely to be able to overcome many of the legislative barriers that overseas markets presented, so the new car had to be designed with modern safety features in mind. Maybe even the fitting of impact-absorbing bumpers.

Warner also believed that the market for cars such as the Seven was becoming more sophisticated and that sales could be won by offering a car with traditional Seven qualities combined with a higher level of comfort and much improved weather protection. He also subscribed to the view that a manufacturer should have a graduated range of models, the idea being to capture the buyer at a young age with the inexpensive 'nursery slope' Seven, then as his income increased, convert him to an Elan, followed by a Plus 2 and thereafter progressively provide whatever larger and more expensive models Colin Chapman had up his sleeve. While Chapman himself did not share this belief in a graduated range, every S4 Seven that left Hethel had a sticker on the windscreen that read 'Lotus Motoring Begins Here.'

Quite obviously the list of criteria for the new Lotus Seven that Warner presented to his designers was a long one. But above all else, the car had to look at least something like the old one. After all, Warner had only been given permission to revise the S3, not design a new model...

Peter Lucas and Alan Barrett began work on designing and building the first S4 Seven in March 1969. Lotus Components

Image making. 'Lotus Motoring Starts Here' was how Warner saw the S4's market niche, hoping that he would attract well-heeled young customers who would subsequently graduate to more expensive models in the Lotus range.

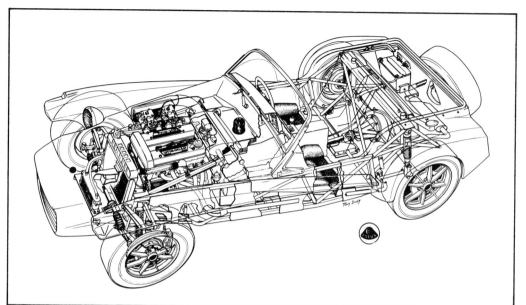

The basic concept of the S4 was like that of the earlier Sevens, but many details of its execution were changed, as this cutaway drawing reveals. Visible here are the leading and trailing links of the rear suspension, with the lower right-hand link triangulated for lateral location, and the Elan-style wishbone IFS. The cockpit tub and main body sections were bonded to form a single unit bolted to the chassis, leaving only the tilt-forward bonnet/nosecone and the front wings to be added separately.

were at that time still located in the main Hethel building and although less was being seen of Colin Chapman on the factory floor, he still walked through from time to time.

'A Chapman visit would raise the temperature of the factory by ten degrees,' said one former employee who also recalled the chilling Chapman 'Black Look' that would be forthcoming when he saw something he didn't like. 'If you'd done a messy weld and put a bit of rag over it to hide it, you could be sure Mr Chapman would lift it and see what you were hiding.' Designers, maybe days into a painstaking drawing, would often find Chapman leaning over them saying 'No, no, no...do it like that,' scrawling the changes over the drawing in marker pen.

Mike Warner decided to take steps to make sure that the bulk of work on the revised Seven did not get interrupted - even by Colin Chapman. A false wall was erected at the end of the workshop and behind closed doors Lucas and Barrett got on with the job. They had completed their work just seven months later. Warner remains adamant that Colin Chapman did not see the S4 until the day it was presented to the Board. Colin Chapman

himself said in 1978: 'I was so busy with other things that I more or less left Mike Warner to run the business on his own and he did this as a sort of secret project out the back.'

The presentation of the Lotus 60, otherwise known as the S4 Seven, took place in October 1969 in one of the hangars on the Hethel airfield. Three prototypes had been built up and the sheets were due to be drawn back at 9.00am. Graham Nearn was invited personally by Warner to attend. When he arrived a few minutes before the appointed time, Colin Chapman and his wife Hazel were already there, along with Fred Bushell, Graham Arnold, Mike Warner and other interested parties.

Proceedings had begun early and Nearn recalls that everyone was standing around shuffling their feet, not knowing what to say. Mike Warner remembers clearly Chapman's reaction upon seeing the car. 'He turned to Hazel and said: "Christ Hazel, they've built a new bloody car."' Warner then pointed out that it wasn't really a new car, just a development of the S3 and that anyway it was a surefire success. Graham Arnold, in his inimitable fashion, was attempting to jollify the occasion but only succeeded in making things worse by poking fun at aspects of the car's styling. Then Fred Bushell landed Graham Nearn on the spot by asking: 'Well Graham, do you think you can sell this for us?' Momentarily at a loss for words, Nearn managed to regain his composure sufficiently to make some encouraging noises but deep down he wasn't absolutely convinced.

Although he had been a regular visitor to Hethel since Caterham Cars had become sole distributors of the Seven, Nearn hadn't seen the new car before the unveiling ceremony. When he heard that a revised car was on the way, he had prepared another proposal as to how the car should be developed and sent copies to the Lotus Board members. 'I thought they were simply going to make a bigger S3,' says Nearn. 'I told them it should have more space, better weather protection and more standard fittings. When I actually saw the car I got quite a surprise.'

This slightly awkward ceremony notwithstanding, productionizing of the S4 went ahead with Chapman's permission. However, the relationship between Chapman and Warner became decidedly frosty and the two had several shouting matches. Warner was one of the few people prepared to shout back at Chapman! Warner: 'Colin and I hadn't spoken for weeks when one morning we drew up together in the car park, he in an Elan Plus 2 and me in an S4 Seven. He looked across for a moment, stared at me, then came over and said, "Well I suppose if we're going to build the bloody thing I'd better drive it."'

There followed five very high-speed laps of the Hethel test track with Chapman thrashing the Seven round the bends on full opposite lock while Warner, cowering in the wind-blasted passenger seat with his notebook, attempted to scribble down the comments shouted across to him. 'It was quite extraordinary really,' says Warner. 'In those few laps he picked up 25 points we were already working on improving and ten others that we should have been.'

The S4 was shown in public for the first time at the Geneva Show in March 1970 but there had been a launch to British journalists at the Grovesnor Hotel in London the previous month. This had been a slightly strange affair because Warner, who had been due to make the presentation, walked out of a Lotus Board meeting held before the press conference. Colin Chapman and Graham Arnold were left to host a somewhat impromptu event that started with Chapman standing up and

The press launch of the S4 took place at the Grosvenor Hotel in London and the event saw a big turnout of media people and Lotus-associated personalities including Graham Hill, seen above posing with the new car and below, discussing its merits with Graham Nearn of Caterham Cars.

73

Colin Chapman and Marketing Director Graham Arnold, seen here making hasty notes, had to improvise the speeches after the walkout of Mike Warner from the board meeting which preceded the S4 launch. Below, Lotus MD Fred Bushell tries the new car for size, finding that the extra cockpit space and legroom make it much more comfortable than earlier Sevens.

announcing: 'As usual with Lotus, no-one knows what's happening!' Some weeks later, Warner reappeared at Hethel and production of the S4 started at last, based around a well organized flow-line with potential for turning out up to 15 units per week.

The lines of the new Seven were indeed reminiscent of the earlier versions, but it was longer and wider. Peter Lucas had designed a simple new spaceframe with spot-welded flat steel sides to the cockpit and engine bay and a folded pressed steel front crossmember. This straightforward design did not have the torsional rigidity of the original Seven and relied upon the fixing of the body to boost its strength.

For the bodywork, engineer and stylist Alan Barrett switched from aluminium to glassfibre construction. He designed a single piece bath-tub cockpit which bonded to a self-pigmented outer skin, the complete unit then dropping into the new chassis where it was bolted into place on bobbins. Glassfibre flared front wings attached to the sides and reached right back to the integral rear wings. A large one-piece front-tilting bonnet completed the bodywork. All the necessary light housings and the air scoop were ready moulded in the body. Even the scuttle and facia were integral. Four sets of moulds were made in total and production of the body units was undertaken by the glassfibre department of Lotus Cars. It really was a very clever piece of design and largely overcame the cost problems of the S3 that the value-engineering exercise had revealed.

Arch Motors were awarded the chassis contract but a company called Griston Engineering stood by to make chassis and fittings in weeks when Arch were overloaded. Such were the numbers being produced by Arch that a special trailer was constructed to deliver the chassis ten at a time to Hethel.

The mechanical makeup of the S4 was very similar to the S3, using cheap mass-produced major components, mostly of Ford origin. Although retaining the Escort axle, Peter Lucas opted for an alternative method of location in an effort to overcome the breakages that required the axle in the S3 to be reinforced. He replaced the A-frame with a pair of fore and aft Watts linkages with the arms at the top going rearwards and those at the bottom coming forwards to the chassis from a welded turret on the axle. At the lower offside was a triangulated arm for lateral location in a manner harking back to the S1 Seven of thirteen years before. The Watts linkages were mounted on big rubber bushes to allow for the conflicts of geometry on bumps inherent in such a set up. Without the bushing the axle would have acted like an anti-roll bar under certain conditions. At front and rear there were coil spring and damper units.

Lucas abandoned the Twelve-type front suspension for the S4 and used instead the double pressed steel wishbones of the Europa without the provision of an anti-roll bar. This was mainly because these components were cheaper and were readily available in the factory parts bins.

The braking system was the same as on the S3, but the Triumph steering rack was replaced by a Burman rack-and-pinion with a Triumph collapsible steering column. The range of engines specified for the S4 also harked back to the S3, with basic 1,300 and 1,500cc Ford units and the option of Holbay modification. The Lotus-Holbay Twin Cam remained as the most powerful variant.

The S4's exhaust pipe ran along the side of the car, as before, although now it was covered by the full-length wing. Fitting the 1,300cc engine to the S4 presented something of a problem because this particular engine had the oil pan at the rear of the sump rather than at the front like the larger unit. This rear-mounted pan fouled on a chassis tube and the solution adopted was simply to cut out the offending tube. Maybe it's just as well that not very many 1300 S4s were built!

The frontal appearance of the S4 echoed that of the S3, with the headlamps free standing. On early S4s, the front indicators were mounted on the sides of the nose, but the moulding was adjusted on later versions to house the indicator units on the wing tops behind the sidelights. At the rear, horizontally mounted light units bolted straight to the flush back panel on either side of the spare wheel. In true Seven tradition this bolted on behind and doubled as a bumper!

Internally, the S4 offered more space than the S3 and drivers of over 6ft found themselves at long last able to get comfortable in a Seven. The seats remained non-adjustable except on export models but they were better formed and arranged than before and gave improved support. Improved weather protection had been a major aim of the S4 and a new hood and sidescreen system was devised. The sidescreens hinged on the windscreen as before, but for the first time had perspex sliding panels. Weathershields of Birmingham were commissioned to design this weather equip-

The S4 was bodied in glassfibre around a steel framed and panelled chassis. The bonnet was a substantial one-piece moulding that pivoted forward to expose the engine, a standard Ford crossflow in this case.

ment for the S4, including the windscreen extrusion, and they produced a new hood to suit, although the initial batch didn't fit. As this was the only item holding up the release of the first batch of cars, three engineers from Lotus Components were despatched to Coventry with instructions not to come back until the

The S4 was undoubtedly a clever piece of design and styling which succeeded in its main aim of making the car cheaper and easier to produce. The facia was part of the main body unit, as were the rear wings.

Better weather protection was high on Mike Warner's list of requirements for the new model and after initial problems the Weathershields-designed equipment worked well. Sliding perspex windows were a novelty for Seven enthusiasts.

The S4 broadly retained the style of earlier Sevens but the simple elegance of line had been lost. Nevertheless, the car was greeted favourably upon its announcement.

Early S4s had the indicators mounted on the sides of the nose as shown here but for later versions they were moved to become integral with the front wings.

weather equipment had been sorted out. This was duly done.

The motoring pundits who were let loose in the new Seven liked it greatly, even with the most basic 84bhp 1600GT Cortina engine. Acceleration to 60mph in just over 8 seconds and a top speed of 100mph meant that this version of the S4 was just as exhilarating to drive as many Sevens before. If it was skittish in the wet and deflected by bumps, hadn't Sevens always been like that? The sensible instrumentation and neat interior, plus the more generous legroom and comfortable seating were generally judged as plus points over the old car. In fact just about every road test of the S4 was, on balance, favourable.

The Twin Cam version tested by the US magazine, *Car and Driver*, managed to top 116mph, although the dash to 60mph still took more than 8 seconds. Customers in the States were asked to pay a hefty $4,336 dollars for their Seven at the time of the *C&D* test, while in the UK the initial price for the Twin Cam was £995, with the GT at £895. As with earlier Sevens, the UK cars were sold in kit form to avoid dreaded purchase tax.

It soon became clear to Graham Nearn that Caterham Cars could not handle the number of cars that Mike Warner was hoping to produce and he agreed to the ending of the sole distributorship arrangement. Warner then set about establishing a new dealer network around the UK. Six such dealers were established, each having made an undertaking to take 15 cars per year, which in itself represented a useful firm sale for Lotus Components.

However, Warner's plan to set up such a dealer network was not instigated without internal problems at Lotus. He wasn't convinced that Lotus Sales would market the Seven in the way he wanted. 'Initially we put Sevens into our normal dealers,' says Warner. 'But they were under pressure to shift Elans and what they were doing was using the "cheap" Seven to get the customers into the showroom and then giving them the soft sell and turning them onto an Elan instead.' It certainly appeared that Sales Manager Graham Arnold was marketing the S4 Seven much more as a 'fun car' than as a serious member of the Lotus range, where it might be seen as an Elan competitor.

In the end, Warner made a direct appeal to Colin Chapman to take over the marketing of the Seven from Lotus Sales. Discussion followed and eventually Graham Arnold agreed to this on the basis that Lotus Racing (as Lotus Components was by then called), would also take back all the accumulated stock of unsold Formula Fords.

So Warner got what he wanted and Lotus Racing started turning out Sevens at a higher rate than ever before. In the best week, no fewer than 15 kits were despatched. The Formula Fords that Lotus Racing now found given back to them did however present something of a problem. But with the design talent within the company this was soon resolved by revamping the bodywork of the 61 to become the 61M. Around 60 units were shifted in this way. However, 50 or so FFs still hung around and they were consigned to storage in a nearby hangar.

Some time later Colin Chapman wandered into this particular hangar reputedly looking for somewhere to store over-produced Elans. Upon seeing the cache of racing cars he commanded, 'Get this floor clear,' so Mike Warner arranged for the racing cars to be stacked neatly against the walls, where they remained for many months!

Once Warner had the marketing of the Seven under his control, he started to promote the car with a more glamorous image than before. Advertising shots of the Elan had shown it in front of the fashionable London nightspot Annabel's. Warner had the Seven photographed in exactly the same setting.

Graham Nearn's acquiescence in Warner's establishment of the dealer network, and indeed his suggestions as to whom some of those dealers should be, stemmed as much from a desire for

Warner saw the 'new' Seven as a much bigger seller than the S3. He thought it would extend the appeal of the car beyond hardy enthusiasts and aimed to promote the car in a more glamorous manner as shown in this period advertisement shot.

self-protection as it did from a feeling of altruism. His 14 years of dealing with Sevens made him doubt that the sales figures aimed at by Warner could ever be achieved. This is even allowing for the fact that the S4 was indeed selling to owners who had previously rejected the Seven as being too impractical and crude. If sales targets weren't met with six other dealers around the country, Nearn could honestly say: 'Well, it wasn't my fault.'

After the initial razzamataz associated with the launch of the new model, sales of the S4 continued at an encouraging level, certainly at a higher level than ever before, if not quite as high as hoped, and it seemed that Warner's plans were being proved right. Forgetting for a moment that the development budget had been greatly exceeded, the S4 was making a profit of £150 per car for Lotus Racing.

However, some new customers were having problems. The owner of a Seven had traditionally carried out much of his own servicing but many of the 'new crop' of customers, people who might otherwise have bought an MG Midget or a Triumph Spitfire, wanted their cars to be serviced by a dealer and some of those appointed were not geared up to do this properly. Some buyers were also finding that this Lotus Seven was not quite what they expected. It was most certainly civilized by normal Seven standards, but compared to most mass-produced sports cars it was still fairly basic. Cars were returned because they leaked or rattled; and people weren't satisfied upon being told that not much could be done about it!

There were also some difficulties with the S4's behaviour when driven hard. The lower-powered versions didn't suffer too many problems, but owners of examples fitted with Twin Cams or Holbay-modified Ford engines found that the car had trouble putting that much power on the road. Under savage acceleration, the rear axle started tramping in the most alarming fashion, while in hard cornering the inner rear wheel would lift off the ground completely. However, it should be said that the majority of S4 owners were tremendously enthusiastic about their cars and loved driving them.

Traditional Seven enthusiasts were initially dubious about the new car but it was soon accepted in the fold by most. However, there were exceptions among the extreme hardcore, as Mike Warner discovered when he went to a Seven Club meeting at the Feathers pub at Ware in Hertfordshire. 'A group of S2 owners spent the whole evening haranguing me. They accused me of totally spoiling the Seven by making it comfortable and weather-proof; a car for nancy boys. I was lucky to get away without being lynched that night!'

On the export front, the S4 never went as well as had been hoped. In the USA it was never properly federalized, despite reports to the contrary. In the 'grey' market that existed, many S4s did in fact make it across the Atlantic; most fully built, but with a smattering of kits, too. With transport costs, build costs and local taxes, Sevens always seemed expensive overseas. Fred Bushell explained the problem: 'In 1971, the price of a Seven in the UK was around £1,000 but that translated to nearer £2,000 in the USA. Seven buyers are a fairly close-knit bunch and in the States they tended to read British motoring magazines so they knew how much the car sold for in the UK. They couldn't help feeling they were getting ripped off. For other buyers who might not be aware of the Seven's background and its association with racing, it simply had to be sold on its appearance and utility and when you get down to it, it didn't stand a chance.'

By the end of 1971 it seemed that the black financial clouds that had dogged Group Lotus for a couple of years were at last receding. Team Lotus were having one of the worst seasons ever, but Lotus Cars were turning in encouraging results again after a very bleak period. On the surface, Lotus Racing looked to be in good shape, but the development costs of the S4 were coming home to roost and there were still unsold cars around.

Coincident with an impromptu stock check and assessment of Lotus Racing's financial position instigated by Colin Chapman, Mike Warner, despite being hotly tipped as the next Chairman of Group Lotus, finally decided that he'd had enough. As if to make sure that there was no going back on his decision, he sent a press release to Reuters announcing his resignation and at 5.10pm on April 6 left his office for the last time. His departure was so sudden that he didn't even take with him his own S4 Seven, complete with BRM-built Lotus Twin Cam.

John Standen was installed in Warner's place as head of Lotus Racing for what amounted to a winding-down operation as the decision was made to stop building customer racing cars. The new racing models due for release in 1971 were dropped and the staff of Lotus Racing started to be moved across into other parts of the company. Assembly of the Seven continued falteringly

S4 on test with *Motor* magazine. They called it a 'Ton-up Lightweight', but thought it was a bit pricey at £1,042 in component form including extras. With 84bhp the Seven managed a best speed of 108mph and 60mph in 8.8 seconds. Note the later-style front indicator mountings.

before finally being moved across to the main Lotus Cars factory in late 1971.

The Seven kit car no longer really fitted in with the Lotus image. Colin Chapman had the Porsche/Ferrari market clearly in his sights and the presence of a £1,000 kit car reminded people rather too clearly of how Lotus had begun. In July 1971, the decision was at last made to kill the car off but Lotus were to continue construction until the large stock of chassis and parts had been run down. The last Lotus Seven left Hethel in October 1972. In two years, almost 600 units had been built. It took the S2 four years to reach this total so the S4 can hardly be judged to have been a flop.

CHAPTER 7

The Caterham connection

Caterham Cars

Anthony Crook now runs that prestigious British luxury car manufacturer, Bristol. However, back in the 1950s he was involved in a less glamorous end of the motoring world, operating as Anthony Crook Motors in a place called Caterham, Surrey. His modest premises were on top of Caterham Hill in a road called Town End. The business comprised a small forecourt and service bay. Behind were a house and a row of lock up garages. In the largest of these garages, Crook's mechanics prepared his Cooper Bristol racing cars with which he made quite a name for himself as a driver.

When Crook decided to move on to pastures new in 1959, a group of partners took over the business, renaming it Caterham Car Services, to sell sports cars and continue with the Esso petrol franchise on the forecourt. One of the five was Graham Nearn, late of the timber trade, and another Ian Smith, journalist, author, leading light of Club Lotus and friend of Colin Chapman. The other three were Mick Carter, David Holmes and Alec Bromley.

It was Ian Smith who suggested that it might be a good idea for Caterham Car Services to become one of the new 'Lotus Centres' that he knew Colin Chapman was in the process of establishing to sell Elites and Sevens. He arranged for Chapman to visit Caterham and the deal was done. Soon after, Caterham took delivery of an Elite kit and a Seven kit which it was their obligation to have available as an appointed Lotus Centre. Spares backup did not enter the equation at that time. Graham Nearn: 'It was simply a question of here's a couple of cars, get on with it. It was never a proper marketing operation. We were never asked how many cars we could sell or asked for any kind of sales forecast or anything like that.'

In fact there seemed to be little relationship between the number of cars that were being sold and the number that were being made. For the first few years it just happened to be about right. Then the market took a downturn and Lotus were left with unsold Sevens in the yard at Cheshunt and chassis littering Panshangar. Hence the £100 price cut announced at the 1961 Racing Car Show to bring the cost of the basic Seven down to a mere £499. Graham Nearn learned of the cut when he walked past the Lotus show stand. 'Oh yes, we've been trying to get you on the 'phone all day,' said a sheepish Peter Warr.

Not only was the price cut associated with a cut in dealer margins to £20 but Lotus were also to start selling direct again. This left all the Lotus Centres out in the wilderness and one by one they moved into other spheres. However, Graham Nearn was determined that Caterham Car Services should stay with the Seven and set about establishing the company as the UK's leading Seven specialists. Right from his first encounter with the Seven, Nearn had recognized the car as a classic design. 'It seemed to me right from the start to be the ultimate small sports car; it didn't seem worth bothering with anything else.'

Caterham still sold the occasional new Seven but concentrated on the second-hand Seven market and set up a spares department for the first time. Mindful of the difficulties in obtaining insurance and finance that people commonly encountered when buying a Seven, Nearn also set up deals with an insurance company and a finance house to offer suitable facilities to prospective purchasers. The company also took on an Austin-Healey franchise and sold Sprites and big Healeys.

This was how Caterham Car Services looked in 1960, a tiny forecourt with swing-arm pumps and workshop behind. More than a quarter of a century later the forecourt still sells Esso petrol but it is somewhat different!

Caterham Car Services' workshop with the Elite and Seven that the firm, as one of the first Lotus Centres, was obliged to stock. The Speedwell Sprite record breaker just happened to be on display when this photograph was taken.

A view of the Caterham Yard in the early 1960s, cluttered with Sevens, Sprites, a Turner and some more mundane saloons passing through the coachworks side of the business which was the mainstay for many years.

Then in 1962, the government removed Retail Price Maintenance from petrol which had hitherto been sold at standardized prices. Caterham Cars saw a petrol price war on the horizon and falling profits from their Esso agency and soon after decided to sell the forecourt to Esso. The partners who owned Caterham Car Sales split up and Graham Nearn took over sole ownership of the premises behind the garage to carry on business. The breakup of the Caterham partnership was marked by a house-smashing party in the cottage that stood on the edge of the forecourt. Esso were due to demolish the house to extend the forecourt and Graham Nearn started the party by throwing a chair through a window. 'The whole party came to a standstill,' he recalls, 'but no-one else wanted to join in...!'

Left to his own devices, Nearn established a car body repair business, Caterham Coachworks, which became the true foundation of the business, upon which its future prosperity was based.

Fellow Seven enthusiast and racer David Wakefield joined Nearn in 1964 to run this side of the business, while Nearn got on with buying, selling and servicing Sevens.

The business continued in this vein right up to the time that

Advertisements for all the appointed Lotus Centres appeared at the front of the magazine *Sports Car and Lotus Owner*. Caterham pioneered the fitting of a 105E engine into the Seven and the resultant car became their demonstrator.

Caterham continued selling and servicing Sevens, ultimately becoming sole UK outlet for them in 1967. Colin Chapman stopped to chat with Graham Nearn on the Seven stand at the 1969 Racing Car Show. Lotus author and former partner in Caterham Car Services, Ian Smith is right of centre in this shot.

Lotus moved from Cheshunt to Hethel in 1966. It became clear that while no decision had been made to drop the Seven, Components simply hadn't started building it again after the move. Graham Nearn was understandably concerned and at the Racing Car Show in January approached Colin Chapman directly. Chapman seemed surprised that a demand still existed for the car and told Nearn to contact David Lazenby, who was at that time running Components, to see what could be done.

Having received the go-ahead from the highest authority at Lotus, Graham Nearn attempted to make contact with Lazenby who proved to be rather elusive. Everyone else he contacted passed him on to someone else. And then on March 27, Graham Nearn's first son was born. He went to the office feeling he could

do anything and decided to ring Lotus just one more time. He got through to Sales Manager Graham Arnold who said: 'It's David Lazenby you want to speak to and he's sitting right in front of me; I'll pass you over.' A meeting was arranged and Nearn's trusty Aston Martin DB2/4 wheeled out and driven to Wymondham for an historic appointment.

Lazenby explained that Components were heavily committed to building Formula Fords but there were sufficient parts in stock to build 20 S2 1500 Sevens. Nearn was happy to purchase them there and then. Thereafter, production of Sevens started to build up steadily once more. Nearn's suggestion that Caterham Cars be the sole distributor of Sevens in the UK was timely and suited Lotus admirably. It meant that Sales Manager Graham Arnold didn't have to worry about marketing the car. An agreement was reached, and from 1967 until the advent of the S4, all Sevens except those sold overseas, passed through Caterham's hands. There was no binding committment as to how many cars Caterham would guarantee to sell. Arnold recognized that Components weren't in a position to make more than four per week and this was just about the level at which sales averaged out.

With Graham Nearn now a weekly visitor to Hethel to collect the week's quota of cars for delivery, it was appropriate that he should become more and more involved in the marketing of the Seven. When he offerred to act as resident Seven specialist on Lotus show stands, Graham Arnold just couldn't believe it. He'd been looking for someone to answer the endless questions about the Seven that enthusiasts still asked and here was someone offering to do it for nothing!

At the 1968 Lotus Open Day Graham Nearn discovered that David Lazenby had left Lotus Components and that Mike Warner was now in charge. He met up with Warner who hinted at some of the ideas that he had for the future of the Seven. This prompted Nearn to prepare and deliver the first of his proposals to the Lotus Board regarding the future of the Seven. Warner also wanted to firm up the production arrangements for the Seven and asked Nearn for the first time to produce a monthly schedule of the number of cars that he would need. Under Warner's regime, Components always produced the required number of cars on time.

Warner was anxious to inject some zest back into the Seven and followed up the introduction of the S3 with preparing both the Seven S and the SS. Both of these were displayed at Motor Shows, marking the Seven's return to such events after a lapse of several years. There followed the dropping of the S3 and the introduction of the S4 along with the establishment of the new dealer network. As compensation for losing the exclusive right to sell Sevens and also in payment of an outstanding commission of £2 per car that hadn't been paid for three years, Warner gave Nearn two cars, including the first S3 which was by then a well-used demonstrator. Nearn, for reasons outlined in Chapter 6, was quietly pleased to see the sales network expanded.

With the introduction of the S4, Caterham Car Sales continued to buy, sell and service the earlier cars. Peter Cooper had been running the service side of the business for some time and

GROUP LOTUS
CAR COMPANIES LIMITED

NORWICH NOR 92W   Wymondham 3411
Telegrams Lotus, Norwich   Telex 97401

19th July, 1971.

Graham Nearn, Esq.,
Caterham Car Sales,
36/38, Town End,
CATERHAM-ON-THE-HILL,
Surrey.

Dear Graham,

Whilst it is still at least eighteen months away, this letter is to confirm that when we discontinue the manufacture and sale of the Lotus 7 from the factory here, we will give you first option to purchase these operations. This would, of course, include handing over all necessary drawings, specifications, body tools, chassis manufacture jigs, etc., etc., and coming to an arrangement on spare parts, etc.

In view of your past and present association with the Lotus 7 I am sure you will be in a far better position to take over this operation when the time comes than any other organisation that might be interested, and we will be pleased to give you every assistance to see that this becomes a reality.

Yours sincerely,

Colin Chapman.

Having persuaded Lotus to keep the Seven going, Graham Nearn was dismayed to learn of plans to drop the model and started lobbying to take over production of the car. Colin Chapman was happy for things to develop in this way as revealed in this letter of July 1971.

found that with the S4 there was much more work, simply because a higher proportion of the new owners were prepared to pay for servicing rather than doing it all themselves.

Then in early 1971, with the S4 in full swing, Mike Warner left Lotus and the coming of the end of the Lotus Seven seemed only a question of time. At this stage, Graham Nearn approached

Colin Chapman to sound out the possibility of Caterham Cars taking over the manufacture of the Seven. Chapman appeared to like the idea in principle and in a letter dated July 19, 1971 said: 'Whilst it is at least 18 months away, this letter is to confirm that when we discontinue the manufacture and sale of the Lotus Seven from the factory here, we will give you the first option to purchase these operations.'

Meanwhile the S4 continued to be produced by Lotus Cars, but without any real enthusiasm. The imminent introduction of value added tax put the final nail in the coffin of the Seven as far as Lotus were concerned. The new Elite and the Esprit weren't far away from entering production and there was a general desire for a clear up of old stock. It was then that Graham Nearn judged the time right to go back to Lotus and attempt to tie up a deal. All his previous approaches had been greeted with a singular lack of enthusiasm, despite Chapman's initial encouragement. At this time Graham Arnold had moved over to the Lotus Boat division so Colin Chapman brought back former Sales Manager John Berry as a 'freelance' salesman and one of the tasks he was given was to sort out the debris left after the closure of Lotus Racing and sell off all the old stock.

A priority on Berry's list was to get rid of 54 Formula Fords; the very cars that Mike Warner had propped up against the walls of the Hethel hangar when told by Chapman to 'clear the floor'. Many of these were in a dilapidated state, covered in bird droppings and with brake fluid corrosion on the chassis where the master cylinders had leaked. Berry asked Nearn if he had any interest in the Formula Fords. Nearn certainly was interested, but only if this deal could be linked with another involving taking over the Seven. However, problems over the terms of the deal for the Seven made the discussions drag on until John Kelly took over as Lotus Service Manager. He was anxious to get on with fitting out for the new range of cars and he pushed for the deal to go through.

Eventually a draft agreement was worked out and much commuting between Caterham and Hethel ensued. Fred Bushell had at last warmed to the idea of Caterham taking over the Seven and agreed to give more information about the car's production costings which did not make altogether encouraging reading as so much of the car had been bought-out and prices kept low against bulk orders. The whole parts supply position was clouded by the fact that some helpful soul put all the computer records relating to

At last the deal was struck in June 1973 and at a ceremony at the Pub Lotus in London Chapman gave the official hand-shake to Graham Nearn for the benefit of the assembled photographers.

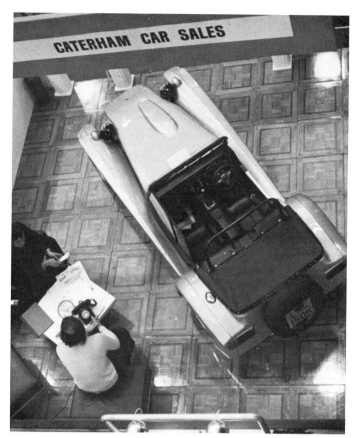

Caterham Cars, operating as Seven Cars Ltd, began by producing S4 Sevens with the Lotus Twin Cam engine, an example of which is seen here on the Caterham stand at the 1972 Racing Car Show. Referring to the car as the Seven Twin Cam Lotus emphasized the link with Lotus although the Lotus badge could not be supplied on the Caterham-built cars.

suppliers – addresses, prices, parts numbers, ordering schedules etc – into a shredder on the basis that as the Seven was on the way out the paper work wouldn't be needed any more...

By May 1973, Nearn was convinced that the project was viable and Lotus were happy with the deal that had been worked out. Under the terms of the deal, Caterham Cars paid an undisclosed sum to take over not only the whole Seven operation but also the Formula Fords and more than 50 Lotus Twin Cam engines. The deal was spread over six months with a penalty if Caterham hadn't completed their part of the deal in that time.

Caterham Cars were not alone in wanting to perpetuate the Seven. A New Zealand firm called Steele Brothers, whose prime business was the assembly of lorries and earth-moving equipment, engaged in fruitful negotiations with Lotus and emerged with two sets of S4 moulds and jigs and a three-year licence to produce the Seven in New Zealand. The Steele brothers ran into problems and the project faltered early on, but not before several dozen cars had been produced. A much revised version of the car was produced with a 2-litre Lotus engine but was stifled by domestic legislation and the high build price.

As part of the deal that Graham Nearn negotiated with Lotus, it was agreed that Colin Chapman would attend an official handover ceremony and also that Lotus would design a new badge for the Caterham-built car. A new badge was needed because the terms of the agreement meant that Caterham could not use the Lotus name, mainly because of worries over the product liability position of a product bearing the Lotus name but not produced by Lotus. Caterham could call the car the Seven, but not Lotus Seven. An artist at Lotus came up with a very simple design reminiscent of the traditional Lotus badge, but bearing the numeral '7'. This gave the closest association possible, without actually calling the Seven a Lotus anymore. This badge was used on the last of the Lotus S4s as well as the Caterham-built cars to emphasize the continuity of the model.

The formalities took place in June 1973 at the Pub Lotus in Primrose Hill, north London. This remarkable establishment was a brainchild of Graham Arnold's. He negotiated with Charringtons to fill a pub with Lotus artefacts ranging from tables made out of Brand Lotus wheels to specially mounted Europa seats at the bar. There was even a 'Seven Bar' and it was there that the handover ceremony took place. Colin Chapman duly turned up and spent the whole afternoon chatting about cars and motor racing, after giving Graham Nearn the 'Official' handshake for the benefit of the assembled photographers.

Once the excitement of becoming a manufacturer had subsided, Graham Nearn and David Wakefield sat down at Caterham to set about putting 'their' car into production.

CHAPTER 8

A new era

Caterham Sevens 1973 to date

There is little doubt that had the Seven been taken on by a company as an isolated project, it would have failed. It was quite simply not self-supporting and when he first considered embarking on the project, Graham Nearn knew that it would not be viable in its own right for several years, even allowing for Caterham's long association with the car. Until then it needed to be run with minimal direct overheads. With the steady and profitable Caterham Coachworks business running well, the Caterham Seven project had breathing space in which to establish itself. The new business was officially called Seven Cars Ltd but was still generally known simply as Caterham Cars. Seven servicing and second-hand sales carried on in parallel with the new project and there were of course all those Formula Fords to find homes for.

The agreement with Lotus said that initially Lotus would supply complete kits of parts for the Seven until Caterham were in a position to source them themselves. However, the loss of the computer records threw Lotus into disarray and complete kits were never forthcoming, although all the stock items held at Hethel were moved down to Caterham. There was a lot of work to do before the first Seven could be built at Caterham.

Dave Merritt was taken on as foreman in charge of building Sevens. He found that chassis were no problem. Arch motors had never stopped making them and it was simply a case of delivering them to Caterham rather than Hethel. Lotus were able to supply the glassfibre body panels while other parts came from stock or simply through persistence with suppliers. Already it was becoming apparent that suppliers that had been happy to supply items in multiples of 100 were less than happy when Caterham

Cars rang up and asked for just ten.

Within two months the first Seven was ready, having been assembled in the workshop at the bottom of the Caterham yard in which Anthony Crook's racing cars had once been prepared. This first car was fitted with one of the batch of Twin Cam engines that Lotus had agreed to supply and was identical to the Lotus-built Twin Cam S4s, except for the absence of 'Lotus' on the badge. The car was simply called the Super Seven; not the Caterham Super Seven at that stage. 'That name just happened,' says Graham Nearn, 'it's not the one I'd have chosen.'

With one car per week being built at Caterham, Graham Nearn set about divesting himself of the Formula Fords which were still in store at Hethel with the proviso that they were gone within six months of the May handover. The sale of these cars was achieved with considerable marketing finesse. Recognizing that many people would like to buy a racing car but were unable to raise the finance, Nearn set up a readily available finance deal that made even uncompetitive Lotus chassis seem appealing! Those cars that had deteriorated too much were refurbished by a company called Group Racing Developments (GRD) run by none other than Mike Warner, late of Lotus Cars. In this way, the bulk of the cars were shifted and the remainder went in a special deal with Motor Racing Stables at Brands Hatch.

But as far as the Seven was concerned there were problems on the horizon. The price of oil had shot up, inflation had started to climb along with interest rates and Prime Minister Edward Heath was squaring up for a confrontation with the miners. Industry generally was beset with unrest and the knock-on effects were being felt at Caterham Cars. The parts stock that had come

from Lotus was being exhausted and it was becoming more and more difficult to find alternative sources. The final blow came when there was no weather gear left. Weathershields of Birmingham had a patent on the mouldings for the windscreen and weather equipment of the S4. The final quota of the original run had gone to Steele Brothers in New Zealand and Weathershields were uninterested in restarting production. Unless, of course, Caterham could place a big order, which meant a minimum of £50,000. Clearly this was out of the question with the number of units Caterham were making. At one point it was even suggested that Caterham should buy the billets of aluminium from which the weather gear was made but this was dismissed as impractical. In the end the fact had to be faced that the S4 had to come to the end of the road. There was no shortage of demand, even in the pits of that particular economic depression. It seemed that there was only one way to go and that was back to the S3.

It was announced through the regular advertisement in *Motor Sport* that 'a limited run of 25 S3 Sevens was to be built.' As Graham Nearn recalls: 'The telephone never stopped ringing. All that remained was to produce the cars.' As a matter of

courtesy, Graham Nearn went to Hethel to tell Fred Bushell what was happening and Bushell agreed that it was the right thing to do.

The time could not really have been worse, with the miners on strike and Edward Heath refusing to give in to their demands, placing the country on a three-day working week in the process and introducing electricity rationing due to shortages of coal at power stations. Such problems notwithstanding, Graham Nearn's co-director David Wakefield was particularly enthusiastic about re-introducing the traditional-type Lotus and outlined the plan. Peter Lucas, formerly of Lotus, was brought in to explore ways in which the chassis could be improved. Service Manager Peter Cooper, working with Ron Davies, set about putting easy-sounding theory into practice.

Working quite literally by gas lamp during the power cuts, the two depanelled a standard S3 chassis produced by Arch Motors and held in the spares department, and set about uprating it to Twin Cam SS specification by adding triangulation to the engine bay and cockpit sides. The aluminium cladding was then refitted with the area around the gearbox mounting strengthened by the

The front end of JPE 946N, Caterham's first press demonstrator, which was tested by *Autocar* in 1975. All the early Caterham S3 Sevens were fitted with Lotus Big Valve Twin Cams that had been acquired as part of the deal whereby Caterham took over the Seven.

addition of a steel plate. The new car was to be fitted with a Big Valve Lotus Twin Cam and this presented a problem.

Even on the original Seven SS models, the Twin Cam had been a tight fit; indeed it rubbed against the underside of the bonnet and parts of the nosecone had to be cut away to clear the carburettors. But now it was discovered that the extra height of the 'Big Valve' lettering cast into the cam covers was sufficient to mean that the engine simply wouldn't fit under the standard bonnet and nosecone. There was no alternative to raising the bonnet line and remoulding the nosecone accordingly. Arthur Francis, Manager of Caterham Coachworks, built a buck for moulding the new nosecone and Peter Cooper fashioned the revised bonnet which gave the necessary clearance.

The beauty of the S3 was that most of the components were of simple design and could be sourced relatively easily, harking back to Colin Chapman's original concept of a straightforward, easy-to-build sports car. Caterham Cars already manufactured glass-fibre wings for the spares department so it was an easy matter to make more for the new car. Likewise the propshaft, instrumentation, wiring and most other fittings were either held in stock or obtained fairly easily. The Twin Cam was mated to the normal Elan-type Ford 2000E gearbox and the rear axle came from the Ford Escort. One of the few problems was finding a suitable radiator but judicious reference to a parts book revealed that the unit from a Hillman Avenger was exactly the size and capacity required. The new car was fitted with Brand Lotus wheels and Goodyear tyres and at the rear was distinguishable from the Lotus Twin Cam by the fitting of top-mounted three-in-one Britax lights rather than having the lights recessed into the wings.

The first Caterham S3 was complete and running by April 1974. Peter Cooper was first to drive it and his first reaction was that the engine had run its bearings. The Big Valve Twin Cam was running without air filters on the twin 40 Dellorto carburettors and the general resonance under the bonnet produced a loud intake 'thump' that was only diminished when air filters were fitted. Apart from the intake noise, the overall feeling was one of

The Big Valve Twin Cam was a tight fit in the Seven and the line of the nosecone and bonnet had to be raised slightly to give clearance.

great enthusiasm for the new car.

Arch Motors still held the Lotus S3 chassis jigs that had devolved to Caterham with the takeover and even during the days of the S4 had still made S3 chassis for Caterham's parts department. So there was no problem increasing the order to cover the new car requirement. By that time, Don Gadd, who had run the Lotus development workshop back in the Cheshunt days, was Manager of Arch Motors and he was delighted to see the S3 revived. The extra triangulation of the Twin Cam SS was adopted as standard for the Caterham chassis but with judicious alteration to some of the tubes to further increase the strength.

The Caterham S3 Twin Cam was officially introduced in September 1974 at a basic price in the UK of £1,540 and the first car, like many to follow, was sold to an enthusiast in Hong Kong. The initial announcement of a 'limited run' of S3s was quietly forgotten about and production steamed ahead. A revised badge was designed by David Wakefield for the Caterham S3s. It was a clever derivative of the Lotus badge that left little doubt as to the model's heritage.

By 1974, purchase tax had been abolished but replaced with value added tax which applied to component cars for the first time. There was also car tax to be paid before the car could be registered in the UK. Even with these forced price increases, the

JPE 946N had blistering performance, with a top speed of 114mph and 60mph reached in 6.2 seconds, and still with the lightning handling response always associated with the Seven.

demand for the Seven was most encouraging and a waiting list immediately sprang up. The introduction of VAT meant that there was no price advantage in buying a kit car, apart from the labour saving aspect, but Caterham elected not to offer the car in finished form in the UK market and concentrated instead on selling complete cars overseas.

The fitting of the 126bhp Big Valve Twin Cam made the Caterham version the fastest Seven yet. The top speed recorded by *Autocar* during their 1975 test was no less than 114mph and they reached 60mph in a remarkable 6.2 seconds. That car was fitted with attractive Goodyear 5½in alloy wheels and G800 tyres and ran with the standard ratio 3.89:1 differential in the Ford axle. The car weighed in at 1,162lb so the power to weight ratio was remarkable, once described by a noted Lotus enthusiast as 'reminiscent of the downfield runners in the 1961 Grand Prix season!' As with most Sevens before, the testers found the roadholding to be superb and the acceleration shattering but were less impressed with the ride quality and found the bump steer alarming at times. But as ever, the final verdict was one of total approval that such a car should still be in production. 'The Seven is not just a sports car, it's the definitive article,' wrote *Motor Sport*.

The first batch of S3 Sevens were all Big Valve Twin Cams but with the demise of the Lotus Europa in 1975, supplies of these engines started to run out. Part of the contract that Graham Nearn had negotiated with Lotus said that Lotus were under an obligation to assist Caterham in the production of the Seven. Mindful of this clause when Twin Cams finally ran out completely in 1976, Lotus announced that they proposed to supply kits of Twin Cam parts to Vegantune, a well-established engine building and tuning company run by George Robinson, where they would be built up into complete engines and then supplied to Caterham. Production of Vegantune Lotus Twin Cams began in 1977.

In the meantime, a Seven had been fitted with a Ford 1600GT Kent engine as a cheaper alternative to the Twin Cam. However, few cars were built to this specification at this stage, but the model would become more significant.

By 1978, when almost 300 Sevens had been built with Vegantune-assembled Lotus Twin Cams, another problem arose because Lotus ran out of engine blocks. Caterham's David

Wakefield set about obtaining supplies of Ford 1600 blocks and Vegantune pressed ahead, building these up with Twin Cam heads to create the 'tall-block' Twin Cam with its modified front casing. The Lotus Twin Cam had been designed around the Ford 1500 block, bored out to 1,558cc, but the 'tall-block' displaced 1,598cc. Both units produced a quoted 126bhp but the

The interior of the Caterham Seven followed the traditional S3 layout although detail changes were made to the instruments and trim.

At speed in the lanes, the Seven's natural habitat. The controls of the demonstrator were identified with simple name tags simply to make things easier for the testers confronted by a collection of anonymous toggles. For regular Seven drivers, identifying the switches soon became second nature.

'tall-block' did this at lower revs and with a slightly lower compression ratio which meant that it was no longer vital to seek out five-star fuel. The first of the new Twin Cams supplied to Caterham was not a success as the compression ratio was too low and the cams too mild. However, after a rebuild to bump up the compression ratio and fit some livelier cams, the new engine revealed itself as a sparkling performer and subsequent units were built to that specification.

Subsequently, this arrangement ran into problems when Lotus ran out of cylinder heads. The situation was getting quite desperate, particularly with the all-important Japanese market where customers wouldn't consider any other power unit than the Twin Cam. At one point in 1978 there were 20 Japanese-spec rolling chassis sitting in the yard at Caterham waiting for Twin Cam engines. Although it was never admitted at the time, there

was for the first time no waiting list. UK customers could enjoy the luxury of same day delivery of a car as a rolling chassis or with a Ford engine. These Japanese-spec cars had such luxuries as dual-circuit brakes and a steering column lock, items not offered on UK-spec cars at the time.

David Wakefield set out to see what could be done about building more Lotus Twin Cams and obtained permission from Lotus to have use of the cylinder head casting equipment at the foundry that had originally supplied Lotus. Caterham managed to conjure up another 53 heads in this way before the foundry was involved in a takeover. Caterham were asked to remove the casting equipment but before it could be collected, Lotus themselves carted it back to Hethel. This misunderstanding was straightened out and Caterham took the moulds over once more. A deal was then struck with another foundry, but their castings

Early Caterham Sevens had no air filters but as production progressed the four gaping carburettor mouths were protected, and quietened a little, by two simple rectangular filters. The bonnet had to be modified to fit round them.

With the increasing shortage of Lotus Twin Cams, Caterham started offering the Ford 1600 GT Kent engine as an option, as per the original S3 Lotus. With 84bhp as standard and plenty of tuning potential, non-Twin Cam Sevens were no slouches.

were of such poor quality that the project ground to a halt. Finally, Lotus changed the policy with regard to reproduction of the engine. They were anxious to safeguard the copyright position of the engine design and there was also concern over the product liability position of engines bearing the Lotus name, particularly in the United States. Technically Sevens should not have been getting into the States but people have always managed to find a way! This time it looked as if the Twin Cam Seven had really reached the end of the road.

As early as 1976, output of Sevens had increased to three or four units per week with the bulk going overseas. Production was at that point moved to the main Caterham workshop. Caterham Coachworks accident repair business was wound down and at last production of the Seven became the mainstay. The workshops where the Seven is still built today are cramped and old. Indeed,

the more romantic among the factory visitors often reflect that it must have been a lot like that at Hornsey in the 'good old days.'

Between 1975 and 1980, apart from the engine saga, the specification of the Caterham Seven changed in many detail respects, generally because of a particular part becoming obsolete or a change of supplier. One significant change introduced early on was that the axle brace was increased in width to take the ends beyond the radius arm mounting brackets. Caterham had found that with grippy tyres and a powerful engine, even reinforced axles could crack unless the brace was extended. In 1977, the normal Ford Escort axle was replaced with that from the RS2000 Escort but this in turn was quickly superseded by a Mark 2 RS axle which gave the benefits of a longer final drive as standard and bigger brakes.

Clive Roberts joined Caterham in 1977 as Production Buyer,

Former Lotus GP driver John Miles demonstrates that a six-footer can fit in the standard Seven without too much discomfort. The steering wheel and gearlever fall nicely to hand, as they say in the trade.

XPE 116S was Caterham's 1979 GT demonstrator, complete with attractive alloy wheels. A compact roll cage was a generally fitted option by this time.

John Miles demonstrates one way of getting out of a Seven with the hood up. It's a job that takes some getting used to but once mastered is quite straight-forward.

The interior of Caterham's compact workshop where at any one time upwards of a dozen cars are on the stocks in various stages of assembly.

With the demise of the Lotus Twin Cam, Caterham set about finding alternative engine specifications for the Seven. By far the most successful has been the Sprint version of the Ford Kent, with twin Weber carburettors, worked head and uprated camshaft among other features which boost power to around the 110bhp mark without temperament.

having previously worked as an engineer for Triumph, and the addition of his practical and theoretical engineering skills to the Caterham team did much to speed up the pace of development of the Seven. Initially change was dictated by the availability of parts, but gradually the philosophy became one of improving the car both for its own sake and for marketing reasons while also attempting to anticipate alterations that would be forced upon the company by changes of parts availability.

Another influential individual who appeared at Caterham at this time was Reg Price, a gifted and intuitive engineer who had built and prepared the famous Modsports racing Seven of David Bettinson. Price was soon contributing to much of the development work on the Seven.

One of the main problems that had to be faced during 1980 was Ford's switching to front-wheel drive for the new generation of Escorts which meant that rear axle supplies would soon run out.

Caterham started casting around for an alternative axle and considered units from Rootes and Vauxhall. But the trouble with these axles was that, unlike that from the Escort, the differential fitted from the rear and not the front. Using a rear-fitting diff

would have introduced problems with bracing the axle, so they were rejected. Eventually the decision came down in favour of a Morris Ital axle, even though it was theoretically weaker than the Ford unit. It also had smaller brakes but did have the advantage of being 30lb lighter and more compact than the Ford axle. It was also slightly wider, so it filled out the wheel arches better. A final plus point was that the Ital axle had the same wheel fixings as standard Triumph Spitfire front hubs. This meant that the front uprights no longer had to be modified and fitted with Ford centres.

In reality there were never any problems with the strength of the Ital axle and the brakes were, if anything, better than those on the Ford unit which had been hindered by a cumbersome self-adjusting mechanism that gave a dead-feeling two-stage pedal.

Another cloud on the horizon that had to be faced was the passing of the Lotus Twin cam. While not giving up hope of resurrecting the Twin Cam, David Wakefield decided that the time had come to produce an uprated version of the Kent engine that would go some way to making up for the absence of the Twin Cam. The occasional new Twin Cam still came to light and many

The Vegantune VTA Twin Cam, based on the Ford Kent block, was listed as an option in the Seven for several years and several dozen cars were supplied with this engine.

The new engine, christened the 'Sprint', was an immediate success, bumping the 84bhp of the standard Kent engine up to a smooth and untemperamental 110bhp while costing considerably less than the Twin Cam. The first car to this specification was built in the spring of 1980. It is interesting to note that the Twin Cam remained listed by Caterham even when there was no realistic possibility of obtaining one.

However, George Robinson of Vegantune had been working on another project during 1979 that held out hope for Caterham and that was the creation of the Vegantune VTA Twin Cam engine. Drawing its inspiration from the Lotus unit, but bearing similarities to the Fiat Twin Cam and the Cosworth BDA, the VTA was quite powerful and made an agreeable noise. Caterham fitted 30 of these units to Sevens before production difficulties at Vegantune brought the project to a temporary halt.

Apart from seeing the introduction of the Super Seven Sprint, 1980 was also the year when supplies of Corsair 2000E boxes ran out. Fortunately the Escort Sport unit was suitable for the Seven and this was duly fitted. To suit the new gearbox, a clever remote control mechanism was devised which gave an improved feel to the change and moved the lever back from the base of the dashboard where Lotus Seven drivers had traditionally skinned their knuckles! A pre-engaged starter was fitted in association with the Escort gearbox and a lighter clutch unit made standard. For the first time this was cable operated and it was altogether more pleasant to operate than the unnecessarily heavy hydraulic system.

In 1981 Clive Roberts and Reg Price started experimenting with a turbocharged Ford engine in a Seven. They installed a Garret AiResearch turbo unit, sucking through an SU carburettor. A smooth 150bhp was produced by this modified engine but although there was plenty of power at the top end, it became very flat indeed at low speeds and this characteristic proved impossible to overcome without an extended development programme. Moreover the amount of power and torque produced by the turbo engine was not significantly greater than a modified, normally aspirated engine and the addition of the turbo made the engine note very un-Seven like. Consequently this interesting project was dropped, but not before David Wakefield had enjoyed the experience of the turbo wastegate sticking closed. This put the boost gauge right off the scale and gave Wakefield

customers fitted second-hand units but the need was there for an alternative. Wakefield, Roberts and Price came up with a simple but effective specification, using a Newman A2 camshaft, gas-flowed head and twin Weber carburettors on a Holbay manifold. The change from the Dellortos of the Twin Cam was necessitated by the fact that they wouldn't fit without modifying a chassis tube in the engine bay. The Webers, on the other hand, fitted neatly although a hole had to be made in the bonnet to clear the air filters.

Caterham celebrated a 25-year association with the Seven in 1984 by producing the silver-liveried Jubilee Seven complete with the highest level of equipment available.

In 1984 the Seven was thoroughly tested by the German motor authorities and granted TUV certification which means that the car may be exported in a finished state to that country. Noise levels and exhaust emissions, plus numerous safety aspects, came in for scrutiny during testing which dictated the fitting of cycle wings and adjustable seats. The GT-engined Seven was found acceptable on all counts.

the most exhilarating run he'd ever had in a Seven!

Another prototype Seven run for the first time in 1981 was fitted with the Ford CVH engine from the new generation Escort. This was simply to see if this engine had potential for use in the Seven in the knowledge that Ford could not guarantee supplies of the Kent engine indefinitely. Running on twin Weber carburettors, the CVH was not rated highly by those who tested it at Caterham. While several owners have fitted CVHs, and find the engine quite acceptable in everyday use, it has not yet been offered as a works option.

Since the legroom of the Seven was very much as it had been when Colin Chapman designed it nearly 20 years before, Clive Roberts' discovery that by repositioning several chassis tubes and relocating the rear seat panel extra cockpit length could be gained, while at the same time increasing chassis stiffness, was warmly welcomed. A contributory factor to this new-found 2½ in of cockpit length was the compactness of the recently introduced Morris Ital differential which left space for the seat back to be moved. As far as Arch Motors were concerned, it was no problem to introduce this variant into the chassis programme. Indeed this

The engine of the German-spec car is the basic single-carb Kent unit, which runs eerily quietly and is astonishingly frugal with fuel.

of time before the steering racks and front uprights that this model provided became obsolete. Clive Roberts modified the rack mountings on the chassis and fitted a regeared Mini steering rack, optimizing the steering geometry as far as possible in the process. Bump steer was reduced dramatically and the feel of the new system was much improved. The front upright problem was solved by negotiating directly with the company that had forged them for Leyland. This particular deal was set up in association with Jem Marsh of Marcos whose cars use similar uprights.

In early 1983 David Wakefield received out of the blue a call from Cosworth Engineering. The gist of this was that Cosworth were putting a BDA-type 16-valve engine back into production and would Caterham be interested in fitting this engine in a Seven? Cosworth were offering to supply complete cylinder head, camshaft and valve kits to be built on to a basic Ford Kent block. The resultant unit would produce around 150bhp easily and much more with tuning. Graham Nearn was immediately enthusiastic. The Seven had strong historic associations with Cosworth and the BDR, as this revised BDA was called, seemed an ideal Twin Cam replacement.

A Super Seven BDR was up and running by early 1984. It managed a top speed of very nearly 120mph and reached 60mph in a shade over five seconds. Here indeed was a worthy succesor to the Twin Cam and the new model was listed at £9,000, making it not only the fastest Seven to date, but also the most expensive.

Clive Roberts and Reg Price had been experimenting for some time with alternative ways of locating the rear axle to obviate the need to brace it. A sliding A-frame with twin trailing links seemed to hold out promise but proved impossible to set up correctly. Then came the news that the supply of Morris Ital axles looked set to dry up by 1986 so the whole future of the live axle was thrown into doubt.

For the first time there seemed to be no other suitable axle. By 1984, nearly every popular car was front-wheel drive and most of those that retained rear-wheel drive had independent suspension anyway. Short of buying the rights to the Ital axle and reproducing it, there seemed no alternative to a major redesign of the rear suspension. Clive Roberts thought that they should aim for a fully independent system but Reg Price was persuasive in arguing for the development of a de Dion rear end. As he pointed out, this would almost certainly be easier to engineer than a fully

was just one of many changes being made to the arrangement of chassis tubes in a quest for even greater stiffness that still continues.

Graham Nearn was naturally delighted with the advent of the Long Cockpit Seven as it offered new marketing opportunities and removed the gripe that many people still had with the Seven; namely not being able to fit into it! The opportunity was taken to develop adjustable seats for the first time although most cars were still supplied with the traditional covered foam bases and backrest.

Triumph dropped the Spitfire in 1979 and it was only a matter independent system and additionally there was historical precedent for the de Dion layout on a Seven.

Roberts and Price set to work. Within weeks a system based around a Sierra differential was conceived, drawn up and the necessary stress calculations performed. It took just one month to transfer the idea onto a chassis. The de Dion tube was located by trailing arms and an A-frame, and the tubework at the rear of the transmission tunnel completely revised to carry the differential. Numerous problems were encountered, but by mid-1984, two prototypes were running successfully. They demonstrated much-improved ride quality and traction, particularly in the wet. The first productionized de Dion was exhibited at the Birmingham Motor Show in 1984. The chassis featured many improvements including the addition of tubes along the sides of the transmission tunnel for the first time. Tests have shown this to be by far the stiffest Seven chassis ever.

In 1984 the Seven was submitted for official testing by the German authorities. After extended development work to ensure that all aspects of the car could pass these stringent noise, safety and emission tests, the Seven was granted its 'TUV' certification which means that it can be sold complete in that market. Similarly the car has been passed by the Dutch authorities and has been judged acceptable in Switzerland too.

Meanwhile, developments were occurring on the engine front. Peter Cooper had built a special Kent engine for a customer who ran a Seven in sprints and hillclimbs. So impressed was Cooper with this specification when he tested it on the road that it was soon agreed to offer it as a general option. And so the 'Supersprint' was born. This pushrod engine, bored out to almost 1,700cc, balanced, with large valves, fully-worked head, Kent camshaft and twin Weber carburettors, produced a lusty 135bhp which slotted in well in the engine range. The idea of boring out to 1,700cc was at the same time carried over to the Cosworth BDR which responded by producing no less than 170bhp on the dynamometer.

The 1,700cc Cosworth BDR makes the Seven exceptionally

Avon Coachworks of Warwick reached an agreement with Caterham to offer a Super Seven 'A' in 1983. Basically this was a mechanically standard Seven with special interior, extra instrumentation, snazzy wheels, spare wheel cover and simple wind deflectors.

A classic profile. This is Caterham's 1985 Motorfair car which went on to become the 1986 press demonstrator. Finished in white with a cream, fully trimmed interior, this de Dion suspension car is quite a head turner and it goes well too, with its 1,700cc Supersprint engine.

The success story of Caterham Cars did not escape the notice of Caterham MP Sir Geoffrey Howe who dropped by in 1985 to try a Seven for size, assisted by Graham Nearn. Previously Sir Geoffrey had had a hand in bringing about the Seven's acceptance in Production Sports Car racing.

fast, and to minimize the risk of such a car being bought by someone unable to handle the power and performance, Caterham have called this version the 'HPC'. HPC stands for High Performance Course and attending a special course devised by Caterham in association with high-performance instructor John Lyons is a condition of purchase.

With Clive Roberts leaving Caterham in 1985, his engineering duties were taken over by Jez Coates, formerly an engineer with Leyland. Working with Reg Price, one of Coates' first projects was to develop a five-speed gearbox option for the Seven, using a modified Ford Sierra 'box. No sooner had this involved project been completed than the pair set about perfecting a 'universal' chassis; one that remains basically the same whether a car is left or right-hand drive, or four or five-speed gearbox. Arch Motors were very glad to move over to making this chassis in mid-1986 as it made their job very much more straightforward!

In 1986, production of Sevens ran at its highest rate since Caterham took over production. With the car available in three forms – basic kit, advanced kit and fully built – an average of five cars per week left Caterham's workshop. The waiting list was also running at its highest-ever level. Proof indeed of Graham Nearn's contention; 'The Super Seven will never die.'

CHAPTER 9

A racing certainty

The Seven in motor sport

From the day that Edward Lewis's prototype Lotus Seven appeared at the Brighton Speed Trials in September 1957 there can hardly have been a weekend when someone, somewhere hasn't taken part in some sort of motor sport with a Seven.

Right out of the box, Edward Lewis's Climax-powered Seven was a winner in the hillclimbs and sprints that he had made his speciality. The car's first outing at Brighton resulted in a second in class which was followed up the next day by a win in the 1,100cc class at Prescott Hillclimb. Lewis had made it clear to Chapman that he intended to run the car in hillclimbs and sprints, areas of motor sport about which Chapman knew little and wasn't particularly interested. Lewis's enthusiasm for these events, though, provided a minimum-effort way of spreading the Lotus word, and Chapman went so far as to enter Lewis under the official Team Lotus banner.

However, Lewis was so impressed with his new car's performance on the hills and in sprints, that he decided to take it motor racing. Before entering a Lotus Seven in a race for the very first time, he sought Chapman's approval. This was forthcoming, but on the basis that the car was entered privately and not under the Team Lotus name. This first event was the popular BRSCC Brands Hatch Boxing Day meeting and Lewis found himself up against some very specialized machinery in the 1,100cc event as his Seven was not eligible for the production sports car race. He didn't win but acquitted himself well. Victor that day was Mike Costin in XAR 11, the works Eleven, despite the fact that Costin was entered as a novice!

Lewis continued to compete regularly with the Seven, replacing the original 1,100cc Climax FWA engine with a larger 1,500cc FWB unit in April 1958. But on its skinny tyres, this very powerful motor was something of a handful by this time. After several 1,500cc class wins, Lewis had a bit of an 'off' at Prescott's Kennel Bend and broke his neck. Lewis: 'The accident was entirely my own fault; the car was taut and sensitive and by comparison with anything else it was a superb roadholder and so responsive. I was trying too hard and doing something I wasn't capable of doing.'

Of the two other cars that were built to the same specification, one went to Club Lotus Competition Secretary Jack Richards and was used successfully in hillclimbs and sprints, frequently beating very sophisticated opposition. One of his best results was during his second season with the car, in the wet at Prescott. He recorded an outright fastest time of the day of 50.6 seconds when opponents including Sydney Allard in the 4½-litre Steyr-Allard and Phil Scragg in his 3½-litre HWM-Jaguar could manage only 53.8 and 52.1 respectively.

The second de Dion-Climax Seven went first to Paul Fletcher and was then sold in June 1958 to Graham Warner of the Chequered Flag racing stable which was associated with his car sales business also known as The Chequered Flag. Warner ran this car alongside an Austin-Healey 100S and an S2 Eleven, the team drivers usually comprising members of staff of his company. The Seven was fitted with a 1,500cc FWB Climax and Lotus F1 wheels and was painted in the team's colours of black and white. It first appeared at Brands Hatch on June 29 in the hands of Percy Crabb who stalled on the line, got away last but drove through the field to finish third.

The obvious form of competition for Seven owners was the

Lewis continued to compete in the Seven during 1958 and 1959. This 1959 photo shows the car in 1,500cc Climax form at Prescott. Lewis fitted the full-width screen in late 1958 in an effort to improve the aerodynamics.

LOTUS

FITzroy 1777

ENGINEERING Co. Ltd

Directors: A. C. B. CHAPMAN, B.Sc. (Eng.). S. P. CHAPMAN, M.Inst.F., A.M.Inst.P. H. P. CHAPMAN

7 TOTTENHAM LANE, HORNSEY, LONDON N.8

AUTOMOBILE AND COMPONENT MANUFACTURERS - RACING AND COMPETITION CAR DESIGN AND DEVELOPMENT

Your ref: Our ref: ACBC.

2nd December 1957.

Ted Lewis Esq.
"Avalon"
The Avenue,
Dallington,
<u>Northampton.</u>

Dear Ted,

      Thanks for your letter of the 28th November and I would, of course, be very pleased to see you competing at Brands Hatch. I would prefer it if in this instance you would enter privately, as in fact you have done on your Entry Form. We will reserve your Team Lotus entries for Hill Climbs only.

      I would like to confirm receipt of the shoes, thank you very much indeed. Sometime I would like to purchase another pair of these in the light colour and do you do a standard with a rubber heel and leather sole and if so I would prefer this set-up.

      Yours sincerely,

      Colin.

MANUFACTURERS OF THE LOTUS CHASSIS FRAME

Edward Lewis's archives yielded up this historic letter from Colin Chapman authorizing the entry of the first Seven in its first ever race.

Lewis again in HNH 577 at Chateau Impney, right. Note the aperture for spare wheel stowage, another Lewis modification.

A third Seven built to a similar spec to those of Edward Lewis and Jack Richards went to the Chequered Flag stable of Graham Warner who painted it in his colours of black and white and fitted it with 'Wobbly Web' wheels as used on contemporary Lotus single seaters.

1,172cc formula sponsored by the 750 Motor Club. But even at this early stage of the Seven's racing career, objections over the Seven were being raised by other competitors. In fact, as early as January 1958, the 750 Motor Club revised the regulations for the 1959 season to exclude all Lotus models except the basic Seven. The statement read: 'The Lotus Mk VI and the Lotus Seven will be accepted if built to the basic standard specification with, of course, the normal 1172 Formula engine modifications. These cars will be ineligible if fitted with de Dion rear axle, disc brakes and similar modifications involving costly proprietary components. The Lotus VI to a standard specification has always been regarded as a car for home building and racing by an amateur and the Lotus Seven in this respect is its logical successor.'

Even restricted to 'basic' specification, the Lotus Seven was more than a match for most other cars in the 1172 Formula. One of the first people to order a Seven for 1172 racing was John Derisley who had already made quite a name for himself racing a 1,172cc Mark 6. He took delivery of his Seven on March 23, 1958 and had completed the build five weeks later on June 1, just in time for the Eight Clubs meeting at Silverstone. He ran-in the

engine by driving back and forth between Camberley and Guildford on the night before the race!

In that first race on June 7, 1958, he was pleased to find that straight out of the box, the Seven was three seconds a lap quicker than the Six. By the next event at Brands Hatch, the Seven had been lowered slightly and close-ratio gears fitted. The result was that he finished as the best placed Seven, pipping Peter Lovely in the 'works' car and attracting the attention of Colin Chapman. He went on to win his class at the Goodwood Members' meeting and rounded off an encouraging start to the season with a class win at the Great Auclum National Hillclimb, winning the Buckler Challenge Trophy into the bargain, always in the past won only by Bucklers!

For the 1959 season, the Lotus Mark 8, Mark 9 and Eleven were banned from 1,172cc racing 'solely on the grounds of their cost.' This left the field clear for the Sevens to start winning outright and the model began to dominate the category.

John Derisley meanwhile decided to indulge in some more rarified competition and drove his car over to Ireland for the Leinster Trophy road race and a sports car event at Phoenix Park.

A successful Seven racer in the early days was John Derisley, seen here in his 1,172cc car at Silverstone in company with a very rare Jowett Jupiter R4, during the 1958 750 Motor Club Six Hour Relay race.

He won his class in both events and returned the next year to finish strongly again, but suffer the loss of all the gears except top. Broken gearbox notwithstanding, the car with no hood and just an aeroscreen for protection had to be loaded up and driven home. To compound the problems there was a dock strike that weekend and the weather was terrible but Derisley set off to catch the only available boat. In Dublin, a runaway bull leapt over the car and caught the driver's head with a hoof. Fortunately, Derisley was wearing his crash helmet in a desperate attempt to keep warm! After overshooting a customs post and nearly getting shot, he made it to the docks 30 seconds before the ramp was pulled up. The weather was no better in Stranraer and the intrepid Seven driver, still with only one gear, picked his way through the fog and rain to arrive home at Camberley some 26 hours after leaving the race meeting. Such was the commitment you needed to go racing in 1959!

One of the best-known early Sevens was the first Super Seven, registered 7 TMT. This car was built up in December 1958 and first raced by Graham Hill at the Boxing Day Brands meeting. In the wet, Hill put his experience and talent to good use and drove the bright red car to win the 1,100cc event outright against much more streamlined opposition. After this success, 7 TMT was designated the factory demonstrator before being sold for £750 to Peter Warr, who became Lotus Sales Manager the following year. He continued to race and hillclimb the car for two seasons. At one of his early events at Silverstone, the fibre timing gear of the Climax stripped and bent all the valves. 'I took the engine to Keith Duckworth,' recalls Warr, 'and he fixed it all up again for £26.' Duckworth himself had aspirations to race a Seven, fitting his car with what he called a 'stage 2½' Climax engine and frightening himself so much with it that he decided to stick to engine building.

Two teams of Sevens, one Ford-powered, the other Climax-powered, ran in the 750 Motor Club's Six Hour Relay race at

Graham Hill got the introduction of the Climax-powered, live-axle Super Seven off on a high note by beating all the streamlined cars in the sports car race at the Brands Hatch meeting on Boxing Day 1958.

Here is Hill making the most of the wet and slippery conditions to lead home the field and score a sensational win in the little car.

Silverstone in 1959. In the Climax team was Peter Warr with 7 TMT while in the Ford-powered team was Warren King with chassis 401, the first production Seven. The handicappers gave the team no chance of winning but the Sevens ran strongly until one by one they were struck down with one failure or another – all except King's car which had to keep circulating way beyond its alotted time while the other cars were repaired. King: 'I'd already done my stint but then had to go out again after everybody else packed in. The temperature gauge started rising and eventually went off the scale. I was resigned to the engine blowing up any minute but it just kept going and going! Eventually I got the signal to come in and pass over the sash. I was very relieved!'

The arrival of the revised S2 Seven in mid-1960 did nothing to decrease its popularity in racing; in fact just the opposite, for with the price cut of January 1961, the cost of Lotus Seven ownership was less than it had been four years previously. Colin Chapman was never averse to giving chosen drivers the 'unfair advantage'

and S1 Seven racer John Derisley was one of these. He received a call 'out of the blue' from Colin Chapman, offering him the use of a works S2 Seven for the 1961 season. Derisley would have to build up the car from a kit and enter it in races under his own name. All Chapman wanted in return was for him to win the Brooklands Memorial Trophy which was awarded annually for the best aggregate of results at Goodwood Members' meetings.

Derisley duly received his kit but was held up for want of the adaptor plate that fitted between the engine and gearbox. The engine in question was a Cosworth-prepared 997cc Ford Anglia unit which was now eligible for the 1172 Formula along with a host of other features hitherto banned by the 750 Motor Club on the grounds of cost. These included modified camshafts and four-speed gearboxes. As Derisley explained at the time, writing in *Sports Car and Lotus Owner*, 'It was fairly obvious that the days of cheap motor racing had passed. It appeared to me that if money was to be spent, it was pointless to lavish it upon an engine

Whoops! An over-exuberant M. F. Goodwin in his 1,172cc S1 Seven overcooks it at Brands Hatch during a 1959 race, while the similarly mounted R. Johnson manages to keep his car on the island.

Willie Griffiths was the Chief Mechanic of Team Lotus for several years before leaving to start his own race preparation company. Among his charges in 1959 was Doug Aitken's Ford-powered Seven, seen here minus engine.

The ex-Chequered Flag 1,460cc Climax FWB-powered Seven, VGJ 4, passed to Betty Haig, seen here hard at work hill-climbing at Shelsley Walsh in June 1960.

The Seven was a mainstay of club sports car racing in the early 1960s, as shown in this 1962 Oulton Park grid with its mix of Sevens, other road sports cars and club-man racers.

112

Sevens went GT racing too, although Tony Goodwin had to fit his car with a Fibrepair gullwing hardtop to qualify. His powerful Ford-engined car is seen here in 1962 up against some considerably heavier opposition.

possessing side valves.'

The new car was christened at the Boxing Day Brands Hatch meeting where teething problems prevented it from showing its real mettle. However, the next time out at the first Goodwood Members' meeting of 1961, Derisley took a storming victory in the scratch race for sports cars. He went on to enjoy a highly successful season in this works car and took it on his by now regular trip to Ireland. On the way back to England after a depressing event spoiled by arguments with the handicappers, Derisley discovered the 'unfair advantage' that Chapman had given him. The car was being tow-started when suddenly the chassis broke in two; two of the main tubes had simply snapped. Upon examination it was discovered that the tubes were not of the standard 18 gauge steel, but ultra-thin 22 gauge metal.

Don Gadd, who worked in the development shop at Cheshunt when the car was built, remembers Derisley's chassis passing through his department. 'We all said it would never work because it was so light, but Colin Chapman assured us that it would be OK; and I suppose it was – just!'

At the end of a successful 1961 season, Derisley found himself in the position of needing to win the very last race in order to make sure of taking the Brooklands Memorial Trophy. Consequently, Colin Chapman offered him the use of the works Formula Junior engine. In the event, Derisley found this special engine performed worse than his normal unit but still went out and won the race and collected the Trophy.

With engines available to suit most forms of club racing, the Seven established itself as the ideal way for the clubman to enjoy himself. The car was sufficiently civilized to be driven to the circuit, unloaded and then raced. It was the perfect introduction to the sport and many aspiring driver took the Seven route. Formula 1 graduates Peter Gethin and Piers Courage both made names for themselves in Sevens in 1962. 1985 and 1986 World Sports Car Champion Derek Bell started his career in a 1,500cc Seven shared with a friend: he won his first event in it at a wet 1964 Goodwood meeting and hasn't looked back since.

The renaissance of French motor racing talent in the late 1960s is largely due to the Lotus Seven. French journalist Jabby Crombac, who had himself raced a Lotus Six some years previously, conceived the idea of Formula France, exclusively for

French drivers, all in Lotus Sevens. The deal he contrived was based around Ford of France buying 21 S2 Seven chassis from Lotus to be distributed among various French motoring clubs. The kits were supplied less engine, gearbox, wheels, tyres and wings but came with a specially-printed illustrated set of building instructions, prepared by Seven fitter Peter Brand. Ford supplied the engines and gearboxes and Michelin came up with the tyres. Club members built up their car which had then to be decorated in regional colours. The club's most promising young driver was nominated to pilot the Seven in a series of races.

Fourteen Sevens were completed in time for the first race of 1964. Roy Badcock, foreman of Lotus Components, went across to France to scrutineer each car before it was allowed on to the track. The standards of preparation ranged from superb to tatty. At least one car was presented with its front wishbones mounted upside down. 'This ended up in a real shouting match,' recalls Badcock. 'They insisted that it was quite safe, despite the ridiculously high ride height. In the end we just refused point blank to let it race until they'd gone away and fixed it!'

Peter Brand assembling one of the Formula France cars during a photo session to produce the assembly guide that was sent to France with each car.

One of the star drivers to emerge from Jabby Crombac's 1964 Formula France series aimed at encouraging French driving talent was Patrick Depailler, seen here racing in the colours of the Auvergne region.

114

Clubmans racing was created to provide sport literally for 'club men' running simple cars in the style of the Seven and no longer able to compete with the increasingly specialized and expensive machinery in mainstream sports car racing. This BRSCC meeting at Cadwell Park is typical of mid 1960s Clubmans action—mostly Sevens with a few specials and limited production racers.

In the end, the racing was excellent and the crowds loved the sight of a bunch of Sevens being hurled around by young Frenchmen. The quality of the drivers to emerge from this series was quite astonishing and included such notables as Cevert, Servoz-Gavin, Pescarolo and Depailler. Depailler, who raced in the Auvergne regional colours, had particularly fond memories of his Seven and wanted very much to own another one. After winning the 1978 Monaco GP he said: 'Now I can afford to buy my car!'

Meanwhile, back in Britain, the Seven in standard form was very competitive but many owners needed to go one better and built special versions; some at least were built by Lotus. Several S1 cars were converted to de Dion suspension. Others were equipped with disc brakes, adjustable front suspension and some even had fully-independent rear suspension grafted on.

Among the first Sevens with independent rear suspension was the so-called Lotus 7½ which was developed at Cheshunt by engineers Hugh Haskell and Don Gadd for the 1962 season. An S1 chassis was strengthened and fitted with adjustable twin-wishbone front suspension. At the rear, full independent suspension was based around an Eleven differential with Lotus 20 hub assemblies. Fitted with a Cosworth-prepared Ford 105E engine, this sophisticated Seven was very fast indeed, if stretching the spirit of production racing somewhat. It raced with great success throughout 1962 and 1963. Even Colin Chapman was inclined to have one of his last competitive outings and raced the 7½ during the 1962 Six Hour Relay at Silverstone.

Another Seven in the mould of the 7½, but a rather more official project, was given the designation type 37 and known as the Lotus Three-7. This car was conceived as a new-generation Clubman racer for the 1965 season. The Clubman Formula had been introduced by the British Racing and Sports Car Club (BRSCC) and British Automobile Racing Club (BARC) in 1964 to provide a championship for cars such as the Seven which were

Hugh Haskell built his Lotus 7½ in 1962 with the aid of fellow Lotus employee Don Gadd. It was strictly for racing and had independent rear suspension, disc brakes and adjustable front suspension without the integral anti-roll bar of the standard Seven. With a full-house Cosworth 105E engine, this Seven was a real flier. Even Colin Chapman couldn't resist having a go in it! Frontal details, right, include the reworked suspension and disc brakes.

John Berry in the Lotus Three-7, the one-off Seven racer that he campaigned in Clubmans events with considerable success.

The Three-7's rear suspension was an independent design based around an Elite differential. The system looked neat but needed considerable development to get it to work properly once Berry decided to race the car.

being outclassed by increasingly sophisticated and specialized mid-engined machinery in sports-car racing. The Formula called for an open-wheeled two-seater with front-mounted Ford engine. 'Standard' Sevens were doing well in the Formula, but Mallock was the dominant chassis. Lotus were winning in just about every other formula and Peter Warr, head of Lotus Components, set out to do the same in Clubmans after Colin Chapman had 'let it be known' that he wanted a car to appear. The prototype was exhibited at the 1965 Racing Car Show.

However, even before Peter Brand had finished assembling the new car, the decision had been made to drop the idea because the cost turned out to be far too high. The Three-7 was a very sophisticated design, with a strengthened S2 chassis, Elite-based five-link independent rear end, double-wishbone front suspension, disc brakes all round and a dry-sumped Cosworth 116E 1,340cc screamer producing 125bhp. The car was exhibited nonetheless and attracted a lot of interest but soon afterwards an official announcement went out that said: 'Because of an increase in orders for the racing Lotus Elan S2 and the special equipment

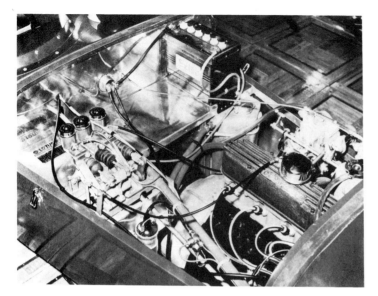

The Cosworth-tuned 1,340cc Ford engine of the Lotus Three-7. The immaculately prepared car was displayed at the 1965 Racing Car Show but no further examples of the model were ever produced officially.

Ford-Lotus Cortinas, the Three-7 has not yet gone into production.' Nor did it.

The prototype was brought back from the show, never having moved under its own power and it languished in a corner of Components' workshop for a period. However, John Berry, Home Sales Manager of Lotus, arranged to take over the car in lieu of sales commission and went Clubmans racing. The Three-7 was an immediate success and became the car to beat for several seasons.

From John Berry, the Three-7 passed to Tim Goss who raced it for two seasons. When Goss approached Lotus Components in 1969 to sound out the possibilities of building him a new Clubmans car, he found Mike Warner very receptive to the idea. Warner was anxious to give sales of road-going Sevens a lift. He also wanted to demonstrate his support for the Clubmans Formula in the face of an attempt to replace it with a new series for mid-engined 'F100' cars. He thought that F100 would be much too expensive for the Clubmans concept and in mid-1969 had issued a statement saying that Lotus would not build a car for the Formula.

From John Berry, the Three-7 passed to Tim Goss, seen here in the car at Brands Hatch in 1968. His enthusiasm was to be the germ of the next Seven-based Clubmans car.

118

The final development of the Seven-based Clubmans theme, apart from the unraced 1971 Racing Car Show car, was the 7X, here driven by Tim Goss at Brands Hatch in 1970, the year in which the combination won the Clubmans Championship. To meet the demands of the increasingly competitive formula, the car had evolved a considerable distance from its Seven origins.

The result was the Martin Wade/Mike Pilbeam-designed Lotus 7X which was completed on Christmas Day 1969 and won its first race by a huge margin at Mallory Park on Boxing Day. Goss went on to enjoy a successful season with the car and, predictably enough, won the Clubmans Championship. To look at, the 7X was decidedly un-Seven-like, apart from the basic configuration, and the divergence increased as it was further developed. Underneath, the chassis bore similarities to the S4 Seven, although the panelling was in stressed aluminium rather than steel. The rear was independently suspended around an Elan differential while the front had Lotus 41 F3 suspension.

The 7X was complicated and sophisticated, but the 'X for experimental' suffix indicated that Components might put it into production. Among the cars on the Lotus stand at the Racing Car Show in January 1971 was a new Clubmans design, billed as a development of the 7X and designated Seven Series 4 Clubman. It had reverted to a de Dion rear end and the brochure offered a rolling chassis less engine and gearbox for around £850. But, as already recounted in Chapter 6, 1971 quickly brought the decision to stop making customer racing cars, and the Clubman

was one of the casualties. The bodyless show car did not reappear.

Meanwhile sports-car racing generally was becoming more specialized; the Seven was no longer the all-round racer that it had been a decade before. Production Sports Car (Prodsports) racing was instigated in 1973 to cater for true road-going sports cars as distinct from specialized sports-racing cars or highly developed Modified Sports (Modsports) cars.

After the changeover of Seven production from Lotus to Caterham, the RAC was reluctant to admit the Seven on to the list of eligible cars for either the Modsports or Prodsports series. However, Graham Nearn was persistent in his lobbying for the Seven to be accepted. For the 1975 season, he was successful and the Seven appeared in the RAC listing of Modsports cars despite resistance from Peter Browning, head of the BRSCC, whose brainchild Modsports had been. It seemed only fair that the Seven should be admitted when cars like Ginettas were considered eligible.

Nearn recalls: 'I argued that the Seven was a production car, a sports car and therefore it was entitled to race; the fact that it was

Director of Caterham Cars, David Wakefield was a keen racer of Sevens and is seen here at Brands Hatch in a Clubmans event racing an S2 fitted with a special three-valve Martin cylinder head on the 1340 Ford engine.

Graham Nearn of Caterham was often seen on the racetrack too. Quite often the car in question would have been 'borrowed' from the Caterham showroom for the weekend and would be back there again on the Monday morning hopefully none the worse for its high-speed adventure.

The Caterham Seven was at last pronounced eligible for British Production Sports Car racing in 1980 and, during the following seasons, many Sevens took to the tracks again. This shot was taken at Brands Hatch in 1983 and shows the front-running Sevens of John Stenning and Maynard Soares harrying the big Porsches.

quick and competitive was just too bad, certainly no reason it shouldn't race.'

Former Seven and Clubmans racer Dave Bettinson was the first to take advantage of this opportunity to run a Seven in Modsports and enlisted the help of engineer Reg Price to construct the car.

The pair took a standard Caterham chassis and lightened and strengthened it. A Holbay Clubmans engine was moved back in the chassis as far as possible and mated to a close-ratio gearbox while the rear axle housed a limited-slip differential. The front suspension was reworked with double wishbones and lower anti-roll bar and rear axle location changed to long radius arms and Panhard rod. The car was shod with the latest F3 rubber.

In the best traditions of racing Sevens, it won first time out, in the wet at Thruxton. Starting from the middle of the grid, Bettinson took advantage of his excellent rain tyres, drove by the rest of the field and won by half a lap. Unfortunately this success brought problems. Other competitors noticed that while the Seven did indeed appear in the RAC list of eligible cars, it was in a separate supplement and not in the 'Blue Book' itself. The letter of the regulations said that to be eligible, cars must be listed *in* the Blue Book. Protests followed and the RAC dithered. Rather than

issuing a definitive statement clarifying the situation, meetings were held and the eventual judgement was that during 1975 the Seven could race, but only if every other competitor signed a piece of paper giving permission. Bettinson pressed ahead on this basis; at most events he managed to get all the signatures but at other events someone would object and the car would have to be loaded up and taken home after a wasted trip.

Bettinson did manage to win his class in 1975 and continued to enjoy four successful seasons with the car which was continually improved by Reg Price. Ultimately it was fitted with a Lotus Twin Cam to replace the Kent engine and the rear suspension redesigned around a clever sliding A-frame. At the end of the 1978 season, Bettinson sold the Seven to Rob Cox-Allison. Unfortunately, during the last race before handing over the car, Bettinson had an almighty accident at Thruxton. The car was destroyed and the deal with Cox-Allison renegotiated. For rather less than the previously agreed sum, Cox-Allison took delivery of the remains of Bettinson's Seven, plus a new chassis that Reg Price had built. Cox-Allison built up the new Seven round that chassis, christened the car 'Black Brick' and embarked on six dominant seasons of Modsports and GT racing.

Meanwhile, Graham Nearn had been stepping up his campaign to have the Seven admitted to the BRSCC Prodsports series. A stroke of marketing genius was coining the slogan 'Too fast to Race' which started a roaring trade in Seven tee-shirts.

Nearn seemed to be getting nowhere with the BRSCC or the RAC. In the end he wrote to Geoffrey Howe, Caterham's MP. The gist of his letter went: 'This is really a question for the Court of Human Rights in the Hague, but I thought I'd better write to you first.' Nearn explained that here was a British car that wasn't allowed to race in a British championship, while Japanese cars were admitted. Geoffrey Howe responded, saying he was looking into the matter, and also wrote to Sir Clive Bossom, head of the RAC. Nearn: 'Suddenly it all happened; we were accepted at long last but they put us in the top class, and restricted us to the basic GT engine, just to be on the safe side.' In fact it had been David Wakefield who had suggested this eventual compromise simply as a means for Caterham to 'get a foot in the door'.

In that first season, Caterham ran a works Seven which was horribly outclassed in the company of Morgans and TVRs. At various times it was driven by Clive Roberts, David Wakefield, Reg Price, Dave Bettinson, Chris Meek and journalist Jeremy Walton. For 1981 the car was moved into its rightful group and started to enjoy rather more success, being joined on the grid by several privateer Sevens.

In 1981, following the adoption of the FIA Group 3 regulations which made Prodsports a much more restricted formula, the under 2-litre class became the preserve of the Seven. John Mayne won his class in the championship that year and John

Stenning did the same in 1982. Also in 1982 Gary White, driving a Seven Sprint, won the Donington Production GT championship outright. Then in 1983, Maynard Soares won the overall Prodsports title, losing out subsequently on a technicality to a Porsche after being pipped in the last race of the season by John Stenning's similar Seven.

In both 1983 and 1984, Sevens took part in Britain's only round-the-clock motor race, the Willhire 24 Hours at Snetterton. In the 1983 event, a three driver team of Maynard Soares, Clive Roberts and the author survived 900 laps of the Snetterton circuit to finish eighth overall and second in class after losing almost an hour during the night to change a split fuel tank. 1984 saw the Seven Drivers Team of John Stenning, Maynard Soares and Gary White finish second in class again after being assaulted several times by saloon cars and having the fuel tank fall out!

1983 also saw a team of Sevens win on handicap the 750 Motor Club's Six Hour Relay race at Silverstone. The winning team of five drivers used the novel technique of running just two cars, one of which circulated totally reliably for five of the six hours, the other car going out only when the primary car came in for fuel and a driver change.

With the demise of Prodsports racing for the 1986 season, the BRSCC moved instead to various one-make series. There is such a series for Alfa Romeos, Porsches and now also one for Sevens. After a tentative start with small grids, this has developed into a highly popular affair. In many ways it sees a return to the old ideals of Seven racing of a quarter century before, as many of the

Dave Bettinson sold his Modsports Seven to Rob Cox-Allison who went on to build several other Seven-derived GT/ Modsports cars that he named Black Brick.

Maynard Soares won the 1984 Production Sports Car Championship overall, having coped with the races being amalgamated with the Production Saloons on occasions during the season which led to some pretty hair-raising moments.

Sevens ran in Britain's only 24-hour race in 1983 and 1984. Driven by Clive Roberts, Richard Cleare and the author, number 33 ran strongly during the 1984 event before being punted into the barriers and retirement by another competitor.

cars that race are in regular use on the road.

In the United States, the history of Seven racing is marked by just as many disputes as have afflicted the car in Britain, if not more. S1 Sevens had not attracted too much attention to themselves and had raced in the modified class of Sports Car Club of America (SCCA) events. However, the advent of the Seven America and then the S2 version marked a change of Lotus marketing policy and many more Sevens started to be seen in the States. People started paying attention.

For 1961, Sevens ran in the waifs and strays class F, but the following year, the Seven America was placed in Production Class G and the Super Seven listed for Class D. In both cases Sevens proceeded to dominate so convincingly that for 1962 the penalty was paid and both Sevens found themselves reclassified against much stiffer opposition. Peter Pulver, an East Coast distributor for Lotus, was behind the annual classification submissions to the SCCA and feedback from him did much to determine how the Seven's specification would change for the following year. The special SCCA 1,340cc engine was a fruit of

Sevens still feature in the UK's premier relay event, the 750 Motor Club's Silverstone Six Hours, winning on handicap in 1983. Here Tony Dron brings in the sash for Gary White to take up the challenge.

With the relaxation of sports car racing regulations to cover 'road-going' cars in 1985, Robin Gray produced his fantastically quick Lotus Twin Cam-powered Seven and cleaned up in just about every race he entered.

this association and in its success lay the seeds of its downfall as the SCCA decided that they didn't want the Seven at all for 1963.

This was big enough news to make the British motoring papers and the report in the April 12 edition of *Autocar* detailed how the SCCA had refused to admit either the Lotus Super Seven 1500 or the Lotus Super Seven Cosworth 1500 because the Lotus factory had not submitted the necessary application forms in time. Lotus themselves claimed to have sent the form on November 22 along with the forms relating to the 1963 Elan, which *had* been included in the new season's listings. The SCCA went further, saying that the Seven did not comply with FIA bodywork regulations or the spirit of club racing. Bearing in mind some of the expensive exotica that was admitted for '63, the 'spirit of club racing' line seemed ridiculous. The whole thing was highly suspect, but as far as the SCCA was concerned, the Seven was not wanted. However, in 1977 it was back in the running and Tom Robertson drove his 116E-powered 1963 car to victory over all the modern opposition in the SCCA National Championship, albeit fourteen years late!

CHAPTER 10

Everyday excitement

Buying and running a Seven

The days of the £500 Lotus Seven are long passed. Sevens are no longer 'student cars' as far as price is concerned. A new one costs around the same as a modern 'hot hatch'. This tends to be reflected in the price of second-hand Sevens. No longer can a neglected Seven be picked up for a few hundred pounds; even a very tatty example will command a sizeable price.

The field of second-hand Sevens is something of a sellers' market. All-told, fewer than 4,500 examples have been made. A high proportion of these survive, but the total is still a tiny number when compared to that of most other classic cars; consequently, at any one time there aren't too many Sevens on the market.

There are also many different specifications of Seven. If you decide to look for one particular type of car, the choice will be even more limited. Prospective Seven buyers do however have one very big advantage over buyers of most other 'classics' simply because Sevens are still available new. Die-hard enthusiasts will argue that early cars are the best, but in engineering and drivability terms, new Sevens must be considered better. However, if you consider that 'character' consists of water leaks, bump steer and ride harshness, then the new cars have less character. If you are six feet or more in height it may be that a later Seven is the only one you can consider. The long-cockpit version certainly opens the doors of Seven motoring to those who would once simply not fit! Metaphorical doors, that is.

Before you go looking for a Seven, you need to decide exactly what you want it for. If you simply desire a car to restore and cherish, the choice is wide. If on the other hand you want an Historic example, possibly for the occasional spot of Historic motor sport, you'll need to look for an S1 or an early S2. If your plan is to go 'modern' racing it will pay to look for as recent a car as possible. This is not simply because of improvements to the chassis design and equipment, but because the newer the chassis the 'tighter' it will tend to be. The rivets of old original cars tend to loosen up and the tubes can decay. This will not only have an adverse effect on the handling but might be dangerous under racing conditions.

Older Sevens do feature strongly in the BRSCC's Seven Championship, but it tends to be the newer cars that win the races outright. Another advantage of owning a more recent Seven is that spare parts tend to be more readily available.

Any Seven is exciting to drive, but some are more exciting than others. The 1172-powered S1s and early S2s were considered brisk in their day but are fairly pedestrian by modern standards. Sevens with A-series engines offer sparkling low-down performance but have a fairly low top speed. Ford 105E-engined cars of similar capacity offer comparable performance but don't have quite the same free-revving characteristics of the BMC-powered cars and use more fuel into the bargain.

Climax-powered Sevens are naturally among the most desirable. With a punchy 75bhp from only 1,100cc, the car is a real flier but relatively few examples of this particular Super Seven were made. The favourite of many Seven enthusiasts is the Cosworth-built 1,340cc power unit which gives the car the benefit of high power and low weight with excellent handling balance. Later Sevens became more powerful but heavier. While the 1,500cc Ford engine offers good solid performance, the more powerful 1,600cc unit offers better performance still with its

A Climax-powered S1 Super Seven restored by Mike Brotherwood of Brotherwood Sports Cars. Such a car might once have been available cheaply but those days are long gone.

The beautifully restored engine bay. Note the quality of the aluminium work which was prepared by Williams and Pritchard who have been associated with the Seven since its inception.

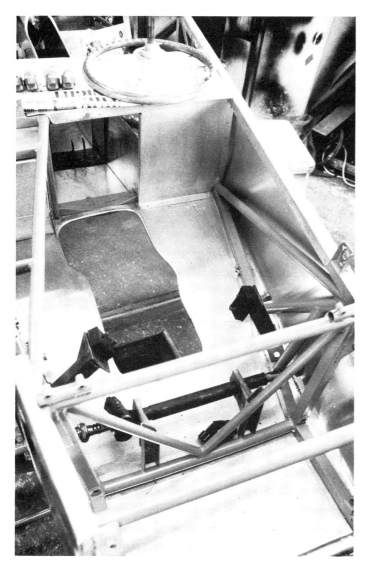

An S1 characteristic is the aluminium undertray which was dropped for the S2. Note the location of the steering rack behind the wheel line.

The S1 undertray also extended under the rear axle where it made access awkward and acted as a mud trap; again, discontinued on later Sevens.

crossflow cylinder head.

At the top of the desirability ratings as far as many Seven enthusiasts are concerned is the Twin Cam Seven. Lotus built only 13 Twin Cam S3 Sevens (plus a handful of backdoor examples). These are clearly identified with SS badging and the implication of finding any other S2 or S3 with a Twin Cam, but without SS badging, is that it is an uprated standard car. It may be that the chassis has been similarly uprated to SS specification but this is seldom the case, so there is certainly a greater risk of experiencing chassis problems.

Most 'genuine' Twin Cam Sevens will be either Caterham S3s, or Lotus S4s. Only the very early Caterham S3s had Lotus-built Twin Cams. Thereafter the engines were built up from parts by Vegantune. In turn the later Vegantune engines had the 'tall' 1600 Ford block which gave a capacity of 1,598cc as against the earlier 1,558cc.

Twin Cam engines offer plenty of power when they are in peak

A period shot of a Seven being built up, in this case with a Ford sidevalve engine. Very few original 1,172cc Sevens survive as most have been 'improved' by the fitting of more recent engines. Similarly, many S1s have been kitted out with glassfibre wings and nose, simply because the original aluminium items are so expensive to replace or repair.

condition, but if a Twin Cam is neglected, performance can tail off significantly. Overhauling a Twin Cam can be expensive; certainly costing more than similar work on a pushrod Ford-engined car. But properly looked after, a Twin Cam can be very reliable.

Many Sevens have enjoyed 'improvement' during their lives. This means that some cars have a dual identity. Quite apart from the possibility of having an engine transplant, a car may have been re-chassised, had a different axle installed, been fitted with flared wings rather than cycle wings, had a later nosecone fitted, or any combination of the foregoing. S1 Sevens in particular have been widely uprated; most often by the fitting of glassfibre wings and nosecone to replace the original easily-damaged aluminium items. Quite a number of S1s have been rebuilt around later chassis but there are a number of tell-tale signs, described in full in Chapter 3. A true S1 Seven should have, among other things, aluminium wings, droopsnoot nose, aluminium undertray beneath the engine and axle, curved radius arms and axle location by a triangulated link rather than an A-frame.

An early S2 can be differentiated from an S1 by the nosecone

A desirable sight and a rare one these days. The cast rocker cover indicates that this engine has been uprated by Cosworth; in this case it's a 105E Anglia unit.

line and the chrome grill: less apparent features include the use of an A-frame and the deletion of the diagonal tubes from the engine bay. Additionally the inner trim panels and facia should be riveted in place rather than screwed or fastened by Dzus.

A late S2 can look alarmingly like an S3, but the crossflow engine, exterior fuel filler and fuel gauge, plus the revised facia with speedo and tacho directly in front of the driver are giveaways. The Ford axle and wider rear wings will not be immediately apparent.

There is no mistaking the glassfibre-bodied S4 Seven for one of the earlier cars. Caterham built 38 S4s before switching to the S3 and these 1973-built cars, which all had Lotus Twin Cam engines, should have the Caterham '7' nose badge rather than a Lotus one. It should be said that many Caterham owners fit Lotus badges, so this is never a reliable indication.

The main consideration when inspecting an S4 is whether or not the chassis is sound. The use of pressed steel chassis sides and front suspension crossmember made rusting a serious problem on Sevens for the first time. The 'bathtub' construction of the S4, with the inner shell sitting in the chassis, gave rise to water and mud traps. Consequently the steel panels of the S4 can rot from the inside out. This generally becomes apparent only after many years and in this respect the S4 is a far better rust-resister than most cars. However, a rusty S4 chassis calls for a major strip down and rebuild. Fortunately, new chassis are readily available and usually represent the most cost-effective way of restoring the car.

S4 Sevens do also suffer from a growing feeling of looseness as the years and miles build up. The car was not designed to have a stressed body but in reality the glassfibre does help stiffen the chassis considerably. The problems arise when the body mountings start to loosen; the whole car becomes floppy. Its handling deteriorates and terrible creaks and groans become a fact of motoring! The difference in feel between a 'loose' S4 and a newly re-chassised example is dramatic.

The life expectancy of S2 and S3 chassis can be remarkably long, but as with any steel chassis, rust and fatigue can take their toll. The tubes in the area of the suspension pick-up points at front and rear are the most likely to fail first. It is well worth spending time in and under the car checking out those tubes that are visible; failure of those that are hidden behind panels will

There's no mistaking the nose of a genuine S1 for that of an S2 as both the grille and the droop of the nose differ. However, if the car has been meddled with, some more fundamental detective work in the region of the axle or steering rack may be needed to establish its true identity. TBY 484's disc brakes are not a standard S1 feature, though original equipment on this special car.

The all-important chassis plate in the engine bay; in this case a modern reproduction but the details it carries are genuine enough. Some Sevens have confused identities because the frame number which is usually hidden on the chassis tube under the master cylinders has mistakenly been taken as the chassis number following the loss of the chassis plate.

The S4 Seven became something of a forgotten car for a time, but interest in this model is increasing and many examples are being restored.

hopefully be shown up during a test drive as the car will probably pull to one side, or lean.

A decayed chassis is far less of a problem with a Seven than it is with almost any other sports car. If it is a localized problem, a skilled restorer can peel back the aluminium, effect a repair by replacing the bad tubes and then rivet the aluminium back down again. However, should the extent of the decay make this partial repair uneconomic, Arch Motors are able to recondition original chassis, or supply, through Caterham Cars, complete replacement units incorporating such recent improvements as are appropriate. As far as S1 chassis are concerned, Frank Coltman, formerly of the Progress Chassis Co, original builders of the S1's frame, is still in business in a small way and can build replacements for these very early cars.

Repanelling a Seven chassis is a job for the skilled restorer. If you are a stickler for originality you may even want to go back to Williams and Pritchard who are still in business in north London. However, the historic reputation of this tiny firm is such that the waiting list is very long. If you want them to tackle a job for you, be prepared to wait. W&P still hold the original patterns

for the S1 aluminium nosecone and wings but these parts don't come cheap when compared to the glassfibre versions. It's easy to see why Colin Chapman changed to the new material with the introduction of the S2 Seven.

The Seven's rear axle is a common weak point, particularly on the more powerful cars. The likelihood of failure is dramatically increased if an early car had been fitted with a Twin Cam, unless the axle has been braced. Bracing was introduced fairly late on in the S2's life and is a modification well worth incorporating on earlier cars. For maximum benefit, the bracing should extend across the full width of the axle and not just across the centre part.

A prime sign of axle distortion is dripping oil which further shortens the life of the A-frame rubber bushes. These hard-worked components start to knock after only a few thousand miles but replacing them is fortunately a simple business.

New Nash Metropolitan or Standard Companion axles are no longer available but are the sort of component that will repay a search of local scrapyards. Additionally in the UK there are enthusiasts' clubs for both Standards and Metropolitans and both organizations can occasionally help with finding parts. You

may have to join up first though! The Ford axle of the S3 Seven can still be found new if you search hard enough, but reconditioned or second-hand units abound. The same is true of the later spec Morris Ital axle used in post-1981 Caterham Sevens: although Caterham do stock these items new, the stock is finite and there will be no more new ones once these have gone.

The beauty of the Seven in being such an effective melange of largely mass-produced components holds true as far as the engine is concerned. Spares for Ford units of 997, 1,172, 1,340, 1,500, and 1,600cc are not hard to come by, nor are they particularly expensive. If the local motor factor can't help, there are car clubs for the Ford sidevalve, Ford Anglia 105E, Ford Classic and Ford Cortina. The situation for A-series engines is possibly even rosier. The engine is still in production, albeit in heavily revised form, but most parts are available 'off the shelf' while in reserve there are clubs for the Sprite, Mini or A35, all of which used the A-series. There is a shortage of Lotus Twin Cam cylinder heads but otherwise, spares for this engine are plentiful from any one of several Lotus specialists.

Gearboxes, brake parts, steering gear and most ancillaries can all be traced to some other donor car for which parts may still be available, new or second-hand. Caterham Cars' own stores department is biased towards the more abundant later cars and most mechanical, body and trim parts are available over the counter or to order.

If, after due consideration, you decide that what you really want is a new Seven, there are three possibilities, all of which mean joining a waiting list. Overseas buyers in Germany, Holland, Japan and Switzerland are in the fortunate position of being able to buy a Seven complete and ready to go. Buyers in the UK on the other hand must complete the car's assembly themselves and register it as 'home-built'.

There are currently two options for the home-builder. The first is the 'starter' kit which resembles the original Seven kit as conceived by Colin Chapman. The basis is a panelled chassis unit that is wired up, has the instruments fitted and the brake lines laid in. To this must be added the various ancillary components which are available from Caterham as supplementary kit packages or can be sourced independently and second-hand if desired.

Using this method it is possible to build up a new Seven for considerably less than the cost of a complete new car. The penalty is having to register the car with a 'Q' suffix on the registration plate. This is because Caterham Cars will not issue a certificate of newness which qualifies it as a new car. However, having a Q-plate does mean that car tax is not payable upon registration.

The second and most popular option for the home-builder is the complete component car. This comes on its wheels, with the engine, gearbox and transmission in place. The engine will have been run and adjusted. Assembly comprises tightening and adjusting the suspension, connecting various ancillaries such as the clutch and the speedo, fitting the trim and hood, wiring up the lights, assembling the exhaust system and cooling system before firing up and making final adjustments. The whole operation should not take much longer than a weekend and requires little more than an 'average' set of tools.

All that remains then is to pay a visit to the local Customs and Excise office with a bank draft to pay the car tax. This is calculated on a formula of which Caterham will advise you. A tax certificate will then be issued which can be taken to the Local Vehicle Licencing Office where you will undoubtedly have to queue to register the car and pay for its first tax disc. It may be that the LVLO requires the car to be inspected before registering it, so be prepared for this further delay. Alternatively, they may decide to issue the necessary papers without such an inspection, in which case all that remains is to obtain a set of registration plates bearing the new number. Once these are fitted, you are free to aim your new car out on to the open road and start to enjoy the fun.

Even in absolutely standard form, a Seven is very exciting to drive. However, should you decide to uprate the car, the possibilities are far-reaching. Every engine ever offered in a Seven has behind it a wealth of tuning heritage; none more so than the Ford Kent unit which has been standard fare in boy-racer Escorts for years and is the basic power unit in both Formula Ford and Clubmans racing.

A gas-flowed head, hotter camshaft by any of the well-known tuning firms such as Kent, Piper, Holbay or Cosworth, plus free-flow manifolding and Weber carburettors, will boost the power output of a standard engine by a significant amount and at quite reasonable cost. Increasing the output of a Kent unit beyond 145/150bhp will start costing a great deal of money with the need to

A Seven kit part-way through assembly. No special tools are needed to build the car, neither do any special skills have to be mastered.

use a steel crankshaft plus special con rods and pistons. The engine will also become very cammy and difficult to drive on the road.

In standard form the Lotus Twin Cam is a potent and tractable engine but there is scope to modify it to produce 150/160bhp

Jobs to tackle include fitting up the exhaust system . . .

. . . fitting the wings and nosecone . . .

. . . and installing the interior

before launching into the sphere of the open cheque book.

However you decide to modify your Seven, make sure that the rest of the car is up to the job. Standard Seven brakes will easily cope with extra power if they are in good condition; likewise the axle, if it is properly braced and otherwise healthy. Before uprating an S2, consider having the chassis improved. Also bear in mind that in years to come, it is good, original cars that are likely to command the highest prices. Replacing a 1,340cc Cosworth engine with a Twin Cam might make the car go faster, but arguably does not make it more desirable.

Should you decide to take your Seven racing, there are certain aspects that will need attention, presupposing that the car is otherwise in tip-top condition. An approved design of roll cage will be needed and the race scrutineers will want to see a fireproof panel round the fuel tank. The car will also need a master switch in the electrical system. A securely mounted four or six-point harness is also vital and, particularly on early cars, fitting such a system will mean welding new brackets to the chassis. As far as tyres are concerned, find out what the other Seven racers are using and, to begin with at least, go for the same.

On the mechanical side, if the car does not already have an oil cooler, it is a worthwhile addition, as are baffle plates in the sump to prevent oil surge on cornering. You will have fun with the car in standard form, but after a race or two you may be drawn to fit adjustable dampers and uprated springs, if you have not already done so. You may also decide to fit an alternative diff ratio to make sure that the engine reaches maximum revs in top.

Thereafter it's a case of setting the car up correctly and driving it as fast as possible. You might consider fitting the demon full-race engine, but beware of what is not permissible under the rules of the race series you're tackling. Bear in mind also that Colin Chapman conceived the Seven as a car that could be driven everyday to work and then at weekends taken to a race meeting or hillclimb and still give a good account of itself.

He would doubtless be happy to know that three decades later the Super Seven is still giving so many people so much enjoyment and shows all the signs of continuing to do so indefinitely.

There are two main ways of getting into a Seven with the roof up, depending on one's agility and inclination, head first or rear first!

The treatment of the Seven's front may have changed in detail over the years, and the tyres grown wider, but the overall impression is the same as ever, simple and unmistakeable.

APPENDIX A

Technical specifications – production models

Author's note: For much of its life the Seven was produced in a fairly informal manner with spurts of production followed by lapses. Introducing hard and fast rules regarding Seven specifications somewhat misrepresents the way in which the car was made, because relatively low production levels coupled to the enthusiastic and accommodating nature of customers for the car tended to mean that specification changes could occur at short notice as the whim of builder, buyer or parts supplier demanded. The following specifications should therefore be regarded simply as general guidelines to Sevens through the years.

S1 LOTUS SEVEN F
Introduced October 1957.
Initially called simply 'Lotus Seven' but became 'Seven F' with the introduction of the Seven A in October 1959.
Engine: Ford 100E 1,172cc four-cylinder sidevalve unit. Bore 63.5mm, stroke 92.5mm. Compression ratio 8.5:1. Single Solex carburettor. 40bhp at 4,500rpm. Higher spec engine available as optional extra included twin SU carburettors, four-branch exhaust manifold, stronger valve springs, polished ports, worked cylinder head and higher compression ratio to give 48bhp.
Transmission: Ford 3-speed gearbox. Close-ratio gears optional extra. BMC Nash Metropolitan rear axle, standard final drive ratio 4.875:1, options up to 5.375:1 or down to 3.73:1.
Suspension, brakes and steering: Independent front suspension as on Lotus 12 — lower wishbones, anti-roll bar and upper links form top wishbones. Live rear axle located by twin trailing arms and diagonal link. Coil spring and damper units all round. 15in wheels. Hydraulic brakes; twin-leading-shoe cast-iron 8in diameter drums front and rear. Mechanical handbrake. First few production cars fitted with Burman worm-and-nut steering box: chassis subsequently changed to accept modified Morris Minor rack-and-pinion unit. Box or rack mounted behind front axle line.
Chassis and body: Triangulated spaceframe of 1in and ¾in 18swg square and round tube. Stressed riveted aluminium cladding. Aluminium wings, nosecone and bonnet.

Dimensions: Length 129in, width 53in, wheelbase 88in, height (hood up) 44in, kerb weight 980lb.
Price: (1957) Basic £690 plus UK purchase tax £346 7s, total £1,036 7s. In kit form £536 (no purchase tax applicable). Export specification £1,267 7s assembled, including purchase tax. Optional extras: tuned engine £31 4s, close-ratio gears £16 10s, non-standard final drive ratio £4.
Notes: 7-gallon fuel tank at rear retained by elastic ropes. No fuel gauge. Hood and tonneau, spare wheel, tool kit and windscreen wipers all optional extras.

S1 LOTUS SEVEN C SUPER SEVEN
Introduced December 1958.
Engine: Coventry Climax FWA 1,098cc four-cylinder light alloy single overhead camshaft unit. Bore 72.4mm, stroke 66.6mm. Compression ratio 9.8:1. Twin SU H2 carburettors. 75bhp at 6,250rpm.
Transmission: BMC Austin A30 4-speed gearbox. Close-ratio gears optional extra. Rear axle as Seven F.
Suspension, brakes and steering: As Seven F.
Chassis and body: As Seven F, but on production versions coolant filler neck in engine bay rather than accessible through nosecone.
Dimensions: As Seven F, except kerb weight 924lb.
Price: (1959) Basic kit £499, engine £356, plus extras £37 to give total of £892. Assembled price £1,546 5s 4d.
Notes: Splined wire wheels, woodrim steering wheel and tachometer standard. Speedometer optional.

S1 LOTUS SEVEN A
Introduced at Motor Show on October 1, 1959.
Engine: BMC A-series Austin A35 or Morris Minor 948cc four-cylinder overhead-valve unit. Bore 62.94mm, stroke 76.2mm. Compression ratio 8.9:1. Single SU carburettor. 37bhp at 4,800rpm. Versions for USA, designated 'Seven America' used basically similar engine from Austin-Healey Sprite with 8.3:1 compression ratio, twin SUs, 43bhp at 5,200rpm.
Transmission: As Seven C.
Suspension, brakes and steering: As Seven F.

Chassis and body: UK version as Seven F. To comply with local regulations, Seven America had full-length front wings in glassfibre rather than aluminium cycle type.

Dimensions: As Seven F except for America version which because of the flared wings was 2in wider. Kerb weight approx 975lb.

Price: Basic kit including engine and gearbox £511 in UK. America version $2,897.

Notes: Seven America had semi-sidescreens, cooling fan, indicators and improved trim.

S2 LOTUS SEVEN A
Introduced June 1960.

Engine: BMC A-series as S1 Seven A. America version had uprated engine of either 948cc or 1,098cc to Austin-Healey Sprite specification.

Transmission: BMC Sprite 4-speed gearbox. Standard Companion rear axle, standard final drive ratio 4.5:1.

Suspension, brakes and steering: Front suspension similar to S1 but using Triumph Herald uprights. Live rear axle now located by under-mounted A-frame and twin trailing links. 13in wheels. Drum brakes, 8in front, 7in rear. Triumph Herald steering rack mounted forward of front axle line, redesigned steering column with shallower angle.

Chassis and body: Revised version of S1 chassis with fewer tubes. Glassfibre wings and nosecone. Nose line lifted and grille revised. Cycle wings in glassfibre initially available but deleted during 1961.

Dimensions: Length 132in, width 58.3in, wheelbase 88in, height 43in, kerb weight 960lb.

Price: (1960) £611 in kit form.

Notes: Hood, spare wheel and wipers now standard. Steel fuel tank retained by metal straps. Battery moved from boot to engine bay bulkhead. Remote coolant filler standard.

S2 LOTUS SEVEN F
Introduced June 1960.

Engine: Ford 100E as S1 Seven F.

Transmission: Ford 3-speed gearbox.

Suspension, brakes and steering: As S2 Seven A.

Chassis and body: As S2 Seven A.

Dimensions: As S2 Seven A.

Price: (1960) £587 for complete kit. Reduced to £499 in January 1961.

S2 LOTUS SEVEN 105E
Introduced October 1961.

Engine: Ford 105E Anglia 997cc four-cylinder overhead-valve unit. Bore 80.96mm, stroke 48.4mm. Compression ratio 8.9:1. Twin SU H2 carburettors. 39bhp at 5,000rpm. Weber carburettors and four-branch exhaust manifold available as extras on Cosworth version.

Transmission: Ford 105E Anglia 4-speed gearbox. 4.55:1 final drive ratio standard.

Suspension, brakes and steering: As S2 Seven A.

Chassis and body: As S2 Seven A.

Dimensions: As S2 Seven A except kerb weight 952lb.

Price: (1961) £499 in kit form.

Notes: Introduction of 105E engine to power the basic specification Seven resulted in the dropping of the Seven A and America.

S2 LOTUS SUPER SEVEN
Introduced mid 1961.

Engine: Ford 109E Classic 1,340cc four-cylinder overhead-valve unit, modified by Cosworth Engineering. Bore 80.96mm, stroke 65mm. Compression ratio 9.5:1. Twin Weber 40DCOE carburettors on special inlet manifold, four-branch exhaust manifold. 85bhp at 6,000rpm.

Transmission: Ford 109E Classic 4-speed gearbox. Standard-Triumph rear axle, 4.1:1 ratio standard, 4.5:1 optional.

Suspension, brakes and steering: As S2 Seven A.

Chassis and body: As S2 Seven A.

Dimensions: As S2 Seven A except kerb weight 966lb.

Price: (1961) £599 in kit form, £681 plus £350 purchase tax assembled. Optional extras included close-ratio gears £40, sidescreens £7 10s, tonneau cover £5 10s and tachometer £17 10s.

Notes: Sidescreens offered for the first time. Special version of the Super Seven for Sports Car Club of America (SCCA) racing had engine further uprated by Cosworth with 10.5:1 compression ratio, special head, pistons, camshaft, etc.

S2 LOTUS SUPER SEVEN 1500
Introduced September 1962.

Engine: Ford 116E Cortina 1,498cc four-cylinder overhead-valve unit. Bore 80.96mm, stroke 72.7mm. Compression ratio 8.3:1. Single Weber 40DCOE carburettor on Lotus manifold. Standard exhaust manifold. 66bhp at 4,600rpm. Cosworth version also listed with 9.5:1 compression ratio, twin Weber 40DCOE carburettors, four-branch exhaust, modified head and camshaft to give 95bhp at 6,000rpm.

Transmission: Ford Cortina GT 4-speed all-synchromesh gearbox. Standard-Triumph rear axle, 4.1:1 ratio standard.

Suspension, brakes and steering: As S2 Seven A except Girling 9½in diameter disc brakes front, 7in drums rear.

Chassis and body: As S2 Seven A.

Dimensions: As S2 Seven A except kerb weight 1,036lb.

Price: Cosworth version £645 in kit form, £695 plus £173 15s purchase tax assembled. Optional extras included close-ratio gears £40, oil cooler £15, tonneau cover £6 10s, indicators £7 15s and heater £17 10s.

Notes: Other improvements associated with S2 1500 included a hood (now in vinyl) with rear quarter lights for improved visibility. Sealed-beam dipping headlights, electric cooling fan and woodrim steering wheel now standard. Indicators offered as option in UK. Exhaust system now full-length to back of car.

S3 LOTUS SEVEN 1600

Introduced 1968.

Engine: Ford 225E Cortina 1,598cc four-cylinder overhead-valve cross-flow unit. Bore 80.96mm, stroke 77.62mm. Compression ratio 9:1. Single Weber downdraught carburettor. Four-branch exhaust manifold. 84bhp at 6,500rpm. Similar 1300 version also available; 1,297cc, bore 80.96mm, stroke 62.99mm, 72bhp.

Transmission: Ford 116E Cortina 4-speed gearbox. Ford Escort Mexico rear axle, 3.77:1 ratio standard, 4.12:1 optional.

Suspension, brakes and steering: As S2 cars but with Girling 9in diameter disc brakes front, 8in drums rear. Front hubs changed to suit Ford wheels.

Chassis and body: Frame as S2 cars apart from changed bracketry associated with new rear axle and revised exhaust system. Wings widened to accommodate wider track of Ford axle and larger tyres on 5½in rims.

Dimensions: Length 133in, width 61in, wheelbase 89in, height 37in, kerb weight 1,210lb.

Price: (1969) £775 in kit form. Optional extras included seat belts £6 5s, metallic paint £25, roll-over bar £14 and oil cooler £15.

Notes: Full-length exhaust system now fitted with silencer under front wing. Fuel filler now through back panel rather than boot floor. Redesigned facia with tachometer standard. Indicators, sidescreens, seat belt anchorages and electric fan all standard. Cortina wheels standard,. Brand Lotus alloy wheels available.

S3 LOTUS SEVEN S

Introduced January 1969.

Engine: Ford 1,598cc crossflow modified by Holbay Engineering. Compression ratio 10:1. Twin Weber 40DCOE carburettors, four-branch exhaust manifold. Modified cylinder head, high-lift camshaft, Hepolite pistons, balanced assembly. 120bhp at 6,200rpm.

Transmission: As standard S3 1600.

Suspension, brakes and steering: As standard S3 1600.

Chassis and body: As standard S3 1600.

Dimensions: As standard S3 1600

Price: £1,600 fully assembled.

Notes: One-off show car for 1969 London Racing Car Show. Featured many extras including full carpets, special paintwork, air horns, leather steering wheel, etc. Holbay engine spec became an option for production S3 Sevens.

S3 LOTUS SEVEN TWIN CAM SS

Introduced October 1969.

Engine: Lotus 1,558cc four-cylinder twin overhead camshaft unit, as used in Elan, Lotus-Cortina etc. Based on Ford 1500 block, chain-driven camshafts. Bore 82.6mm, stroke 72.8mm. Compression ratio 9.5:1. Twin Weber 40DCOE carburettors, four-branch exhaust manifold. Lotus Special Equipment version produced 115bhp at 5,500rpm, Holbay-assembled big-valve version with alternative camshafts produced 125bhp at 6,200rpm.

Transmission: As S3 1600 but with uprated Borg and Beck clutch.

Suspension, brakes and steering: As standard S3 1600.

Chassis and body: Triangulation added in cockpit sides and engine bay. Prototype SS had steel side panelling but production cars had aluminium. New-pattern rear lights recessed in wings.

Dimensions: As S3 1600 except kerb weight 1,258lb.

Price: £1,250 in kit form.

Notes: Interior trim improved. Indicators mounted on sides of nosecone. Rocker switches on dashboard. 13 Twin Cam SS cars produced 'officially'.

S4 LOTUS SEVEN 1300, 1600 and TWIN CAM

Introduced March 1970.

Engine: As S3 Seven, 1300 or 1600 pushrod unit, or Lotus Twin Cam in 115bhp or Holbay 125bhp form.

Transmission: Ford 2000E Corsair gearbox replacing Cortina unit. Ford Escort rear axle, 3.77:1 ratio standard.

Suspension, brakes and steering: Double wishbone front suspension with separate anti-roll bar. Live rear axle located by A-bracket on offside plus trailing and leading links. Coil spring and damper units front and rear. 9in front discs, 9in rear drums. Umbrella-type handbrake mounted on right. Burman rack-and-pinion steering with Triumph collapsible column.

Chassis and body: Complete break from previous Sevens. Tubular chassis with welded steel sides and pressed steel suspension units. Restyled body now all in glassfibre with integral facia and rear wings plus one-piece bonnet and nose. Much improved weather protection including sidescreens with sliding perspex windows. Optional hardtop.

Dimensions: Length 144½in, width 60½in, wheelbase 90in, height 43½in, kerb weight 1,276lb.

Price: (1970) 1600GT £895 in component form. Twin Cam £1,245 in component form. Holbay version £1,265 in component form. Extras included magnesium alloy wheels £42, heater £17, roll-over bar £15, screen washers £3 5s, air horns £4 15s.

Notes: Overall concept of S4 similar to earlier Sevens but changed in almost every detail apart from engine specifications.

CATERHAM SEVEN S4

Introduced August 1973.

After taking over production of the Seven from Lotus in May 1973 Caterham Cars began by assembling S4 Sevens identical in every respect to the Lotus version apart from dropping Lotus badge.

Price: 1300 £1,195, Twin Cam £1,487.

CATERHAM SUPER SEVEN

1974 to date.

The Caterham Seven has been constantly improved and developed in detail since 1974. The principal engine specifications and specification changes are listed here.

Lotus Big Valve Twin Cam: Initially all Caterham S3 Sevens built with this engine in Elan spec with associated gearbox. Capacity 1,558cc, bore 82.6mm, stroke 72.8mm. Compression ratio 9.5:1. Twin Dellorto carburettors. 126bhp at 6,500rpm.

Lotus Vegantune Twin Cam: Version of Lotus Twin Cam assembled by Vegantune. Initially same specification as Lotus-built version. Then changed to use Ford 225E 1600 'tall' block; capacity 1,598cc, bore 80.96mm, stroke 77.62mm; compression ratio down to 8.5:1, same power but greater torque.

Vegantune VTA: Vegantune designed twin cam unit on Ford 225E block, with belt-driven camshafts. Capacity 1,598cc, bore 80.96mm, stroke 77.62mm. Compression ratio 10:1. Twin Dellorto carburettors. 130bhp at 6,500rpm.

Ford 1600GT: Pushrod overhead-valve engine giving 84bhp from 1,598cc; specification as for Lotus-built S3 1600. 1300 version also available, 72bhp from 1,297cc.

Ford 'Sprint': Caterham-modified pushrod Ford 1600. Twin Weber 40DCOE carburettors on Holbay manifold, with four-branch exhaust. Cosworth A2-type camshaft, gas-flowed cylinder head and balanced assembly. 110bhp at 6,500rpm.

Ford 'Supersprint': Pushrod Ford 1600 further modified by Caterham. Bored to 1,698cc. Compression ratio 10.5:1. Kent 234 camshaft. Big valve gas-flowed head and balanced assembly. 135bhp at 6,500rpm.

Ford-Cosworth BDR: Cosworth 16-valve cylinder head with belt driven camshafts on Ford 1600 block. Compression ratio 10.5:1. Cosworth pistons. Twin Weber 40DCOE carburettors, special big-bore exhaust system. 1,598cc version produces 155bhp at 6,700rpm, 1,698cc version 170bhp at 6,700rpm.

Transmission: Gearbox initially Ford 2000E Corsair; replaced in 1981 by Escort Sport unit with Caterham-developed remote control. Ford Sierra 5-speed gearbox introduced as an option in 1986. Clutch operation initially hydraulic, changed to cable with adoption of Escort Sport gearbox. Ford Escort rear axle initially, replaced by Ford RS2000, then in 1980 by BL Morris Ital unit. De Dion rear suspension introduced in 1985 built around Ford Sierra final drive unit with 3.6:1 ratio standard.

Suspension, brakes and steering: Initially as Lotus-built S3. Adjustable Spax dampers made standard in 1980. Brakes revised in line with axle changes from Ford to BL. Outboard-mounted Ford drums at rear on de Dion cars. Herald steering rack replaced in 1979 by regeared BL Mini unit, with geometry modified to minimize bump steer.

Chassis and body: Chassis initially as Lotus-built Twin Cam SS – basic S3 frame with added triangulation in engine bay and cockpit sides. Numerous small modifications subsequently incorporated. Major changes include introduction of long-cockpit version in 1981 with seat back repositioned to give 2½in extra internal length. 1985; chassis redesigned to accommodate de Dion rear suspension. Tubes added along transmission tunnel. 1986; symmetrical chassis introduced with front-mounted radiator. At introduction of Caterham-built Seven, bonnet and noseline raised to house Big Valve Twin Cam engine. Bonnet louvres standard.

Dimensions: Length 131in, width 61in, wheelbase 89in, height 37in. Kerb weight approximately 1,162lb depending on specification.

Price: In component form. Big Valve Twin Cam (1975) £2,196. Sprint (1980) £5,638. Supersprint (1986) £8,700. 1700BDR (1986) £13,393.

Notes: Car initially similar to Lotus-built S3, numerous detail changes integrated during ensuing production. Revised cooling system, dual-circuit brakes, redesigned wiring loom, battery relocated. Larger (10-gallon) fuel tank. Reversing lights fitted, improved interior, adjustable seats optional, revised instrumentation, steering lock standardized.

APPENDIX B

Seven performance figures

Model	S1 Seven F	S1 Super Seven C	S2 Super Seven	S2 Seven A	S2 Super Seven	S2 Super Seven 1500	S3 Seven S
Engine	Ford 1172 with options	Coventry Climax FWA 1,098 cc	Ford Cosworth 1,340 cc	BMC 948cc	Ford Cosworth 1,340 cc	Ford Cosworth 1500	Ford Holbay 1600
Power	48 bhp	75 bhp	85 bhp	40 bhp	90 bhp	95 bhp	120 bhp
Maximum speed	81 mph	104 mph	103·6 mph	85 mph	102 mph	103·4 mph	107 mph
Acceleration (sec)							
0-30 mph	4·7	3·4	2·6	3·6	4·0	2·6	2·7
0-40 mph	7·2	—	4·1	5·1	5·2	3·7	4·2
0-50 mph	11·7	7·0	5·6	9·2	7·4	5·7	5·5
0-60 mph	17·8	9·2	7·6	14·3	9·9	7·7	7·4
0-70 mph	30·7	13·2	10·5	22·0	13·1	10·2	9·5
0-80 mph	—	18·4	14·3	35·0	18·1	13·9	12·8
0-90 mph	—	—	20·5	—	—	17·7	17·9
0-100 mph	—	—	—	35·0	31·0	27·7	—
Standing ¼ mile	20·8	16·4	15·8	19·2	16·9	15·9	—
Top gear acceleration (sec)							
10-30 mph	—	—	—	—	—	—	—
20-40 mph	7·6	—	7·9	—	—	6·2	—
30-50 mph	7·9	—	6·7	—	—	6·0	—
40-60 mph	10·1	—	6·3	—	—	5·5	—
50-70 mph	16·5	—	8·0	—	—	5·8	—
60-80 mph	—	—	7·6	—	—	6·6	—
70-90 mph	—	—	10·8	—	—	—	—
80-100 mph	—	—	—	—	—	—	—
Overall fuel consumption (mpg)	35·6	30	22·9	25-35	19-25	24·8	18·3
Kerb weight	1,008 lb	924 lb	966 lb	960 lb	1,015 lb	1,064 lb	1,204 lb
Test source and date	*Autocar* 1957	*Autosport* 1959	*Autocar* 1961	*Road & Track* 1961	*Road & Track* 1962	*Motor* 1963	*Autosport* 1969

Model	S3 Twin Cam SS	S4 Seven 1600GT	S4 Lotus Seven	Caterham Super Seven	Caterham Super Seven GT	Caterham Seven Supersprint	Caterham Super Seven BDR
Engine	Lotus Holbay Twin Cam 1,558 cc	Ford 1,598 cc	Lotus Twin Cam	Lotus Twin Cam 1,588 cc	Ford 1600	Modified Ford 1700	Cosworth BDR 1700
Power	125 bhp	84 bhp	115 bhp	126 bhp	84 bhp	135 bhp	170 bhp
Maximum speed	103 mph	108·5 mph	116 mph	114 mph	100 mph	111 mph	120 mph
Acceleration (sec)							
0-30 mph	2·4	3·0	2·6	2·3	2·4	2.0	2·0
0-40 mph	3·6	4·5	4·2	3·2	3·7	3·0	3·0
0-50 mph	5·1	6·3	6·0	4·5	5·3	4·2	4·1
0-60 mph	7·1	8·8	8·7	6·2	7·7	5·6	5·0
0-70 mph	9·6	11·8	11·4	8·3	10·7	8·2	7·6
0-80 mph	13·1	16·0	14·8	10·9	14·6	10·0	9·8
0-90 mph	18·8	24·2	19·0	15·0	22·9	13·9	13·1
0-100 mph	—	—	24·5	22·0	—	19·9	18·9
Standing ¼ mile	15·5	16·0	15·8	14·9	15·7	14·6	13·1
Top gear acceleration (sec)							
10-30 mph	—	—	—	—	—	10·3	—
20-40 mph	7·0	7·1	—	6·0	7·1	7·6	—
30-50 mph	7·0	7·2	—	5·9	6·8	7·1	—
40-60 mph	7·2	7·5	—	6·4	7·0	7·1	—
50-70 mph	8·1	7·9	—	6·5	7·8	6·7	—
60-80 mph	9·4	9·3	—	6·7	9·3	6·5	—
70-90 mph	11·2	13·0	—	7·9	13·6	7·5	—
80-100 mph	—	—	—	11·0	—	10·3	—
Overall fuel consumption (mpg)	19·2	26·3	16	28·3	27·1	23·5	26·7
Kerb weight	1,258 lb	1,276 lb	1,300 lb	1,162 lb	1,110 lb	1,196 lb	1,207 lb
Test source and date	*Autocar* 1970	*Motor* 1970 1971	*Car and Driver*	*Autocar* 1975	*Autocar* 1980	*Autocar* 1985	*Classic Cars* 1984

APPENDIX C

Chassis number sequences

Seven chassis numbers: Those official factory records that were kept have largely been lost and the following is taken from those scraps that do remain. The inconsistencies are such that this should be regarded as only the most general guide.

S1 LOTUS SEVEN 1957-1960
400-499 Hornsey built.
750-892 Cheshunt built.
The missing numbers between the two sequences were allocated to other models as the numbering in the early days was in batches. For example, 500-553 were S2 Elevens and 600-615 Fifteens. Additional confusing information is that some numbers between 750 and 892 were allocated to various Formula Junior racers.

S2 LOTUS SEVEN 1960-1968
SB1000-2101 Cheshunt built.
SB2102-2310 Hethel built.
Prototype S2 given working number 999. All cars had prefix SB for Series B, left-hand drive cars with an additional L prefix. Lotus 3/7 given number outside main sequence 37/R/1 in April 1965. As on all Sevens, the frame number stamped on the chassis under the brake cylinder mounting bears little relationship to the chassis number. Confusion of the two is at the root of many identity problems. The prefix B on the frame number indicated a chassis built by Universal Radiators and A/M indicated the builder was Arch Motors. Interestingly enough, SB1000 was not registered for the road until February 10, 1961; A-series engined, it was registered 7 TPE.

S3 LOTUS SEVEN 1968-1969
SC2311-2563.
SC2564-2576TC fitted with Lotus Twin Cam engine; possibly several others exist. Left-hand drive cars have additional L prefix.

S4 SEVEN 1969-1973
2650-2953 Components/Racing-built cars.
2954-3238. Built by main factory.

3501-3538 Built by Caterham Cars.
The precise number built up by the main factory after the demise of Lotus Racing, formerly Lotus Components, is uncertain, but S4 3535 was the last Lotus-built S4 chassis to be delivered to Caterham Cars and can reasonably be supposed to be the final car.

CATERHAM SEVEN 1974 to date
Prototype with Twin Cam   CS3/3550/TCP
Major specification changes and new options introduced at the following chassis numbers:

First rhd production S3	CS3/3551/TCR
First lhd production S3	CS3/3564/TCL
First 1600GT	CS3/3575/16R
First 1300GT	CS3/3580/13R
First Ford RS axle	CS3/3601/TCRS
First Mk II Escort axle	CS3/3612/TCR2
First Mk II RS axle	CS3/3736/TCRS
First Vegantune-built TC	CS3/3643/TCR2
First Sprint engine	CS3/3938/MKRS
First Ital axle	CS3/4002/TCRM
1984 Jubilee model	CS3/4060/MKRM J001
First Vegantune VTA TC	CS3/4077/VCRM/VTA 001
First 1700 Holbay option	CS3/4110/17HRM
First long cockpit	LCS/4140/MKRM
Last Lotus TC	CS3/4164/TCRM
First 1600 Cosworth BDR	LCS/4268/BDRM
First 1700 Supersprint	LCS/4330/17RM
First de Dion suspension	LCS/4477/17RD
First five-speed 'box	5LC/4577/17LD

The following codes have been used on Caterham chassis: CS3; Caterham S3, TC; Big Valve Twin Cam, P; prototype, R; right-hand drive, L; left-hand drive, 16; 1600GT, 13; 1300GT, S; RS axle, 2; Mark 2 axle, MK; modified Kent, M; Marina/Ital axle, VC; Vegantune VTA engine, LCS; long cockpit, BDR; Cosworth 16-valve engine, 17; 1700cc engine, D; de Dion, 5; five-speed gearbox.

APPENDIX D

Useful addresses for Seven enthusiasts

Companies

Lotus Group of Companies
Wymondham
NR14 8EZ
0953 608000

Caterham Car Sales and Coachworks
Seven House
Town End
Caterham on the Hill
Surrey
0883 46666

Arch Motor & Manufacturing Co
Red Wongs Way
Huntingdon
PE18 7HD
0480 59661
Seven chassis builders

Williams & Pritchard
25 First Avenue
Edmonton
London N18
01 807 6559
Aluminium body parts, particularly S1 Seven

Frank Coltman
19 Meadow View
Potterspury
Nr Towcester
Northants
NN12 7PH
Seven chassis building and repairs

Evante Cars (Vegantune)
Cradge Bank
Spalding
Lincolnshire
0755 67369
Assemblers of Lotus Twin Cam

Climax Engine Services
82 Northwick Park Estate
Blockley
GL56 9RF
0386 700631
Coventry Climax engine parts and service

Brotherwood Sports Cars
247 Oxford Road
Calne
Wilts
0249 817338
Historic Lotus restorer, plus S1 parts supplied

Miles Wilkins
Fibreglass Services
Charlton Sawmill
Charlton
Singleton
Nr Chichester
0243 63320
Coventry Climax and Lotus Twin Cam parts, early Elite specialist

Hajime Tanaka
Kiwa Trading Co
Second Yamamoto Building
1-7-7 Yaesu Chuoko
Tokyo
Japan
Caterham Seven distributors in Japan

Chris Tchorznicki
248 Hampshire Street
Cambridge
Mass. 02139
USA
Caterham Seven distributors for East Coast USA

Sports Cars Fredy Kumschick
Luzernerstrasse
6247 Schotz
Switzerland
Caterham Seven distributors for Switzerland

Sports Cars A/S
Oistein Hagfors
Gladengveien
0661 Oslo 1
Norway
Caterham Seven distributors for Norway

Clubs

Lotus Seven Owners Club
David Mirylees
5 Bamber House
Croesyceiliog
Gwent
Wales
NP44 2AR

Club Lotus
PO Box 8
Dereham
Norfolk
NR19 1TE

Historic Lotus Register
Vic Thomas
Badgerswood
School Road
Drayton
Norwich
NR8 6EF

Lotus Drivers Club
Jenny Barton
21 Beauchamp Avenue
Leamington Spa
Warwickshire

Lotus Drivers Club
Chicane
3 Blythe Avenue
Balsall Common
Coventry CV7 7GN

Club Team Lotus
Ketteringham Hall
Wymondham
NR18 9RS

Club Lotus Australia
70 Neville Street
Marrickville
New South Wales
Australia

Lotus 7 Club Germany
Kaiser Friedrich Ring 33
4000 Dusseldorf 11
West Germany

Club Lotus France
La Pelous
72160 Tuffe
France

Lotus 7 Club Luxembourg
1 Cite Kremerich
6133 Junglinster
Luxembourg

Club Lotus New Zealand
PO Box 1249
Wellington
New Zealand

Envoi: the Seven Experience, hood down on a clear day with a clear road and a full tank of petrol. Bliss indeed. . .